WHEN THE SICKLE SWINGS

KRISTEN VAN UDEN

WHEN THE SICKLE SWINGS

Stories of Catholics Who Survived
Communist Oppression

SOPHIA INSTITUTE PRESS
Manchester, New Hampshire

Sophia Institute Press
Box 5284, Manchester, NH 03108
1-800-888-9344
www.SophiaInstitute.com

Sophia Institute Press is a registered trademark of Sophia Institute.

paperback ISBN 978-1-64413-766-6

ebook ISBN 978-1-64413-767-3

Library of Congress Control Number: 2023945818

First printing

Communism tries to steal your property. That's okay, we can handle that. But it tries to steal your soul ...

—A Cuban expat

Dedication

To all victims and survivors of communism, especially those most forgotten. And for those who felt they had no choice.

Acknowledgments

FIRST AND FOREMOST, I would like to extend my profound gratitude to the witnesses who allowed me to write their stories. I hope their testimonies inspire readers to learn more about the diabolical ideology that continues to oppress the world, and to honor the saints, known and unknown, who resisted.

For their incomparable help with translation, interviews, discussions, and logistics, many thanks to:

> Bruno Schroeder, Aramis Perez, Sergio de Paz, Richard Paez, Norman Fulkerson, the clergy and staff of St. Kieran's Parish in Miami and the Shrine of Our Lady of Charity, Sergio León, Brittany Aguilera, Dr. Victor Triay, Rafael Montalvo, Dr. Yuleisy Mena, all the veterans and volunteers of the Brigade 2506 Museum in Miami, Fr. Ben Kosnac, members of Czech & Slovak association of Boston, Christina Moore, and Phillip Campbell.

My gratitude to Dr. Beth Salerno, for supporting an earlier version of this project and facilitating training in oral history, and to all of my professors who helped me hone the craft of researching and writing contemporary history.

To my family for their unwavering help, interest, and humor, and to my fiancé, Daniel, for his support: thank you for always being there.

Thank you to Sophia Institute Press for giving me this opportunity, and to the many media personalities and followers who have expressed excitement about the project. I look forward to talking with all of you.

Contents

WHEN THE SICKLE SWINGS

Introduction

FOR OVER HALF of the twentieth century, across nearly half the globe, the Catholic Faith was either illegal, repressed, or restricted. Since 1917, the atheistic, false messianic doctrine of Marxist communism had found its expression in state powers, whose messages of equality for all soon descended into totalitarianism, slavery, and slaughter.

This persecution, rivaling that of the Roman Empire, did not take place in some distant century, but in our very own lifetimes. The survivors walk among us. The prisons, holding facilities, and other infrastructure of persecution remain—sometimes memorialized and interpreted for posterity, more often repurposed for some banal commercial use or fallen into disrepair. In some countries, like Cuba, these facilities are still in use for their original torturous purpose.

In researching this book, I was privileged to get to know Catholics from all over the world who suffered varying degrees of oppression for their faith. Catholicism is universal. The unchanging doctrine, sacred language, and devotions take on enculturated flavors to bring the many varied peoples of the earth to the truth of Christ.

In a twisted parody, communism is also universal. Its atheistic, antichrist doctrine extended to all corners of its influence, adapting itself to deal with the particular peoples, their cultures, languages, and traditions. Thanks to its central organ of the Komsomol, party members from such far-flung locales as the U.S.S.R, China, and East Germany imbibed the same ideology, hailed the same glorious utopian future, and assimilated their differences through the communist principle of "friendship among peoples."

In the same vein, communism's persecution of the Catholic Church is universal. First implemented in the Soviet Union in the early 1920s, the program against the Church was repeated with stunning similarity in later communist states.

The blueprint of oppression proceeded as follows:

1. **Outlaw the public worship of the Church.** Make Mass attendance illegal, or at the very least discouraged. Reduce Church presence in public spaces: no processions, pilgrimages, or public celebrations.

2. **Round up the clergy and religious.** Confine them to prisons or forced labor camps. Cut or severely limit contact with the Vatican. Especially target the bishops — this will interrupt apostolic succession, ensuring that the episcopal lineage will die out. No bishops, no sacraments, no Church.

3. **Seize and repurpose Church property.** There is no private property under communism. All is owned by the state, to be distributed "to each according to his need." Steal the treasures of the Church for financial gain, and to ensure that the infrastructure of worship is obliterated. In 1920s Soviet Russia, monasteries were converted into prisons for the clergy, combining points two and three.

4. **Control the Laity.** Place social pressure on practicing Catholics — ostracization, lack of opportunities, threat of arrest. Make their daily lives so difficult they will have no choice but to apostatize. Intimidate them with a constant secret police presence. Raid houses to confiscate religious imagery and sacramentals.

5. **Infiltrate**. Gain informants from within. Send spies to secret Church gatherings. Furthermore, infiltrate the clergy to subvert doctrine and influence the hierarchy. Step-by-step, replace Catholic doctrine with the doctrine of communism, and get them to swear allegiance to the state instead of the pope.

Elements of this anti-Catholic agenda are found in each of the stories you are about to read. The persecution of the Church represented a full assault on all fronts: against worship, against hierarchy, against prayer, against beliefs.

✠ ✠ ✠

Just as Catholicism is universal, and persecution is fairly uniform, so too was Catholic resistance to communism universal, in its own way. What these Catholics did was simply live their faith, in the way of heroic virtue that each baptized person is called to. They just happened to be born into circumstances where doing so would earn persecution and death.

From the secret Masses in the prisons of Cuba to the catacombs of Bratislava to resistance in the streets of Brno, these individuals displayed an unwavering tenacity and a willingness to sacrifice for Truth. They will laughingly say, "You don't want to hear *my* story!" thinking themselves unremarkable. Their humility is to their merit. But there is nothing unremarkable in these testimonies. In their lives now and then, they are and were strong, outspoken about the Faith, resilient, and taking nothing for granted.

Several themes emerged that were common to the experiences of everyone I spoke to.

The first is the utmost importance and centrality of the sacraments. The lengths to which faithful Catholics went to partake of the sacraments is a beautiful testament to these outward signs of God's grace, and to devotion to the Real Presence.

The Church went underground in Czechoslovakia, where priests risked their lives to administer the sacraments in secret. In Cuban political prisons, inmates would faithfully recite the words of the entire Mass on Sundays, even when there was no priest present to confect the Eucharist. Sometimes, family members would smuggle the Blessed Sacrament into the prisons for the sanctification and fortification of these white martyrs.

Another common motif is the role of Our Lady. Marian pilgrimages played a significant role in preserving the Faith during these times, in memorializing the martyrs, and even in the actual overthrow of communism.

Nuestra Señora de la Caridad del Cobre guided the Cuban people through their trials. The shrine dedicated to her in Miami continues to serve as a site of pilgrimage for the Cuban diaspora. The Marian pilgrimage in Nitra, Slovakia, undertaken on the feast of the Assumption every year, proved a pivotal turning point in a series of Catholic demonstrations in 1988 that would culminate in the collapse of communism one year later. The Marian site of pilgrimage in Csíksomlyó, Transylvania, was an anchor to the Catholic population of the Hungarian and Romanian communist states. It has become a site of celebration and remembrance.

It is interesting that none of these three shrines were destroyed by the communists. The people I interviewed speculate that the hand of God was protecting these shrines; that the communist authorities somehow understood and coldly respected their dignity.

Our Lady of Fatima warned us that, if left unattended, Russia would spread its errors throughout the world. The bloodbath of communism's destructive century is evidence that it did, in fact, unleash its hellish errors across the world.

But Our Lady did not warn us and then abandon us. She comes to the rescue of her children, time and time again. It's no coincidence that 1988, the year dedicated by Pope John Paul II as a special Marian year, marked the thaw of the communist freeze in Europe.

✠ ✠ ✠

These are only a sampling of stories. There are millions of stories that will never be told. There are millions more that died, along with their authors, under the communist boot. Nor are these necessarily the most "dramatic" stories—many of those have no more witnesses.

Polish dissident writer Sigismund Krzhizhanovksky's fantastical story "The Autobiography of a Thought" traces the journey of a thought—from its genesis in the thinker's head, through drops of ink onto the written page, into thousands of printed copies, and eventually ending as an epitaph on the thinker's tomb.

In a system of totalitarian repression, not all thoughts were given such air to breathe. Thus, much of the true story of what happened exists only in the memories of the eyewitnesses. As the French writer Antoine de St. Exupery says, "When a man dies, an unknown world passes away."

In an effort to ensure that the harsh truths of communism are not reduced to what Solzhenitsyn diagnosed a "poetry under a tombstone, truth under a stone," I seek to give voice to a generation of Catholics whose testimonies have been repressed, ignored, or buried under the weight of time.

These witnesses carry within themselves many fractals of truth, otherwise unknown, unheard, unexpressed. These stories are valuable not only to ensure that the historical record of communism's horrors is as comprehensive as possible, but also as living icons of God's grace in our own time.

Notes to the Reader

Most European countries oppressed by communism also suffered to some extent under the Nazi yoke. While this reality is peripherally mentioned for context, comparison, or when relevant to the story, this topic is beyond the scope of this book. This is not to minimize the horrors of the pagan, inhuman, anti-Semitic and anti-Catholic Nazi regime. Untold numbers of souls in central and eastern Europe, including some of the people in this book, were persecuted under *both* regimes. God keeps track of their sacrifice.

Many millions of people have suffered under communism since its inception. The Victims of Communism Memorial Foundation estimates that over one hundred million people have been murdered by communist regimes worldwide.[1] Mass graves are still being uncovered. We may never know the full toll. Due to this almost indiscriminate suffering, there are many categories of victim — religious, political, or simply those unfortunate enough to be caught in the crosshairs of a corrupt system. All religions were targeted, to varying degrees, by communist regimes.

The Eastern Orthodox and the Eastern Catholic churches became particular targets of the Soviet Union and its European client states. In Czechoslovakia, Eastern Catholics arguably suffered a stricter repression than did Roman Catholics. Their only three bishops were killed, their religious practice and instruction completely banned (no "National Church" facade was established for Eastern Catholics), and their flock left defenseless. Again, this book's focus on the Roman Catholic Church is not intended to minimize the suffering of Eastern Catholics.

Persecution of the Roman Catholic Church took on a particular flavor due to the doctrine of the papacy and the existence of the Vatican as a political power. The Catholic city-state caused paranoia among communist leaders about a Catholic fifth column within their borders, ready to wield foreign political, economic, and military

---

[1] This estimate is displayed on the home page of the Victims of Communism Memorial Foundation, https://victimsofcommunism.org/.

influence. So, Catholics were deemed dangerous not only for their beliefs, but also for their loyalty to the pope and perceived incentive to become foreign spies. We will see the charge of "Vatican spy" leveled against several Catholic clergy and laymen in this book. Therefore, the lines between political and religious persecution were often blurred. Author Felix Corley, in his archival treatise on religious persecution in the Soviet Union, concludes that Soviet persecution of religion, in its official policy, functioned more as a mechanism of control than a theologically motivated program.[2] His research shows that bureaucrats, on the whole, were staunchly atheist, but uninterested in "proving" religion to be false: they preferred heavy-handed propaganda and measures that emphasized the total futility of religion as an enemy of progress. It is as if they could not even conceive of the supernatural as a possibility. But it is this very enforced atheism that is at the core of their evil. Even if done unwittingly, communist apparatchiks served Satan in the propagation of their materialist doctrine, which claimed that God is dead, earth is Heaven, and Christ's one, true Church is a dangerously archaic foe of man.

The motivation of the persecutors takes on different forms in countries that were historically Catholic, where many who became Communist Party members were forced to renounce the faith of their ancestors and turn on their own families. It is difficult to parse the private, internal motivations of any apostate, and certainly of the mass apostasy that allowed such cooperation with evil. Absent introspective insight, the fruits speak for themselves.

The subsequent canonization of many martyrs of communism proves that whatever the state's particular motivation, the witness of these Catholics earned them the crown of martyrdom in God's eyes.

[2] Felix Corley, *Religion in the Soviet Union: An Archival Reader* (New York: New York University Press, 1993).

✠ ✠ ✠

The stories in this book are representative, but not comprehensive. This volume is not a full history of Catholic persecution under communism, a gargantuan task that is still ongoing as new archives come to light and more survivors come forward. In order to write a cohesive narrative, I had to narrow the scope to be able to give full attention to the stories of a few individuals of heroic virtue. Due to space limitations and the availability of interviews and documents, I have focused mainly on four countries: Cuba, Czechoslovakia, Hungary, and Romania. It is my hope that future projects will include voices from other regions where communism dominated, including the U.S.S.R. proper, its other European satellites, East Germany, Yugoslavia, southeast Asia, other Latin American countries, and China.

In fact, I spoke with Catholics from several countries where communism still rages. Due to the ongoing persecution of the Church in their countries, we decided it was best not to include their stories in the book, as speaking out against these regimes can *still*, in 2023, warrant ostracization, prison, or worse.

One of these countries is Nicaragua where, at the time this book goes to print, faithful Catholics are constantly targeted by their government. In March of 2023, the Vatican officially closed its embassy in Nicaragua in response to the ongoing persecution of the Church under the Ortega regime. Throughout his reign, Daniel Ortega has shut down Catholic charitable organizations and colleges, expelled nuns from Mother Teresa's Missionaries of Charity, deported and imprisoned clergy, and forbidden Catholic processions.[3] In the

---

[3] J. P. Carroll and Erica Lizza, "It Is Dangerous to Be Catholic in Nicaragua. Here's How Americans Can Help," *America*, April 11, 2023, https://www.americamagazine.org/politics-society/2023/04/11/ortega-nicaragua-catholic-church-245067.

most recent shocking measure, the regime closed down the nation's seminary. Nicaragua is slowly receding back into its Sandinista past, under which it has been suffering since the communist craze seized Latin America in the 1960s.

The other is China, the best-known example of a severely controlled "state Church." The ongoing persecution of Cardinal Joseph Zen evidences the continued anti-Catholic policies of the Chinese Communist Party. Even in the rural provinces, locals who tend the gravesites of Catholic martyrs from as far back as Chairman Mao's "Great Leap Forward" of the 1950s stay silent about their knowledge. Speaking too loudly about these martyrs, and certainly to a Western author, could place a target on their backs. The same regime that persecuted the Chinese martyrs as "elements of the right," encouraging citizens to "eradicate the poisonous herbs," retains strict control today.[4]

✠ ✠ ✠

"Swing the sickle, for the harvest is ripe." Joel 3:13

The vocation of every Catholic is martyrdom, be it red or white. At our Baptism we die to the world and are reborn in Christ.

When presented with the ubiquitous communist imagery of the hammer and sickle, I cannot help but be reminded of the sickle's scriptural meaning: the means by which the harvest is cut down, the wheat separated from the tares. The sickle of communism acted much in the same way, purifying the faithful as they were cut down as martyrs.

---

[4] Gerolamo Fazzini, ed., *Diaries of the Chinese Martyrs: Stories of Heroic Catholics Living in Mao's China*, trans. Charlotte J. Fasi (Manchester, NH: Sophia Institute Press, 2016), 131.

Communism, atheism, false faith in this world. Or Catholicism, fidelity to Christ and His Church, eternity. This was the choice presented to Catholics then, is presented now, and will be forevermore under different names.

In supreme irony, the communist sickle, purportedly a symbol of collectivism's agricultural plenty, tells us exactly what it is really doing: *"And the enemy that sowed them, is the devil. But the harvest is the end of the world. And the reapers are the angels" (Matt. 13:39, DRA).* When the sickle swings, we must be ready for the harvest.

CHAPTER ONE

The Doctrine of the Antichrist

SINCE KARL MARX published his writings, the Church has condemned communism as an ideology of false messianism in which man usurps the place of God. In his encyclical *Divini Redemptoris*, Pope Pius XI writes: "Communism is intrinsically wrong, and no one who would save Christian civilization may collaborate with it in any undertaking whatsoever."[5]

Communism was condemned as early as 1846 by Pope Pius IX, who later included it in his Syllabus of Errors.[6] Pope John Paul II, instrumental in the collapse of communism, added to the Church's thought, illustrating that communism fails even in its own humanistic aims:

> The fundamental error of socialism is anthropological in
> nature. Socialism considers the individual person simply as
> an element, a molecule within the social organism, so that
> the good of the individual is completely subordinated to the
> functioning of the socio-economic mechanism. Socialism
> likewise maintains that the good of the individual can be

[5] Pope Pius XI, Encyclical Letter on Atheistic Communism *Divini Redemptoris* (March 19, 1937), no. 58, https://www.vatican.va/content/pius-xi/en/ encyclicals/documents/hf_p-xi_enc_19370319_divini-redemptoris.html.
[6] Ibid., no. 4.

realized without reference to his free choice, to the unique and exclusive responsibility which he exercises in the face of good or evil. Man is thus reduced to a series of social relationships, and the concept of the person as the autonomous subject of moral decision disappears, the very subject whose decisions build the social order. From this mistaken conception of the person there arise both a distortion of law, which defines the sphere of the exercise of freedom, and an opposition to private property. A person who is deprived of something he can call "his own," and of the possibility of earning a living through his own initiative, comes to depend on the social machine and on those who control it. This makes it much more difficult for him to recognize his dignity as a person, and hinders progress towards the building up of an authentic human community.[7]

All these writings can be synthesized in a few basic principles:

1. Communism is inherently atheistic.

2. Communism's false, worldly promises echo the false, worldly utopia of the antichrist, as he is described in Scripture, the writings of the saints, and literature.

3. Communism seeks to destroy not only the body but also the soul.

Resistance to communism is difficult, because of its gradual implementation and totalistic nature. The Russian dissident Aleksandr Solzhenitsyn implores readers of his *Gulag Archipelago* to identify even one point

---

[7] Pope John Paul II, Encyclical Letter on the Hundredth Anniversary of Rerum Novarum *Centesimus Annus* (May 1, 1991), no. 13, https://www.vatican.va/content/john-paul-ii/en/encyclicals/documents/hf_jp-ii_enc_01051991_centesimus-annus.html.

in the charade of arrest, show trial, and imprisonment at which they could have successfully "resisted" in using traditional means. Resistance is often characterized by heroic outward-facing actions. But internal resistance—mental, spiritual—is the most important. It is the priority of the soul and the foundation of sanity in times of trial. The ultimate resistance is to hold on to your soul, to keep the Faith, and to die with the name of Christ on your lips, whenever the time comes.

The fundamental operating principle of communism is the utter absence of God from human achievement. It proclaims that humanity can save itself: through science, ingenuity, economic prosperity, and social principles divorced from their ethical roots. That man is in control of his own destiny, has become his own god, a god who acts through the will of the proletariat and its keepers. And that religion, especially as embodied in the institutional churches, is an outdated myth that only serves to divide, impoverish, and enslave the people.

This is the ideology that leads to the Gulag.

But worse, this is the ideology that leads to Hell.

As I have written elsewhere,

> Christ told us that His Kingdom is not of this world. We know that Satan is the prince of this world and that perfect harmony is *only* possible in Heaven, through our cooperation with God's grace and efficacious suffering in this life. Therefore, any earthly utopian project that denies this supernatural reality is hubris, and as destined to fail as the Tower of Babel.[8]

The idea of a worldly utopia, based entirely in this realm with no regard for the next, is literally the gospel of the antichrist.

---

[8]   Kristen Van Uden, "Modern Forerunners of the Antichrist," Catholic Exchange, May 12, 2022, https://catholicexchange.com/modern-forerunners-of-the-antichrist/.

Fr. Robert Hugh Benson, in his 1907 apocalyptic novel *Lord of the World*, describes the person of the antichrist as a charming, successful businessman and wildly popular social star. Twisting Our Lord's words, Benson's antichrist declares, "I come not to bring the sword, but peace." The antichrist will advocate for a false peace, wherein all religions are syncretized into a vague, universal ideal of fraternity. Truth is sacrificed for the sake of worldly goods. All suffering is drowned in earthly pleasures, numbing the conscience.

Sound familiar?

Empirically, no one can deny the devastating effects of communism. Its record of destruction demonstrates it failure, even in its stated aims.

It declares the free market slavery, and then enslaves its own people in work camps.

It declares religion an unnecessary psychological crutch, and then creates its own religion with its own sacred documents, rituals, moral code, and gods to be worshipped.

It sells its soul for an ideal that is never realized.

Like all deals with the devil, selling your soul does not actually win you eternal life.

The promises of communism are the promises of the serpent in the Garden, dressed up in newer, timelier, more sophisticated garb. Yet the most obvious condemnation of communism is that it is overtly, militantly atheistic.

Fr. Vincent Miceli, in his study of the founding atheist thinkers, explains that atheism is not the absence of worship, but the worship of idols.[9] The practice of communism—complete with ritual, pageantry, doctrine, sacred texts, and practitioners—bears strong

---

[9] Fr. Vincent Miceli, S.J., *The Gods of Atheism* (Manchester, NH: Sophia Institute Press, 2022).

resemblance to religious ceremony. From the childlike worship of an all-powerful being who delivers candy, to the more mature worship of party membership, to the grain of incense pinched by collaborators, the actions demanded by the state amount to acts of worship.

In fact, party membership was such a strong aspect of one's identity, and trust in the party so all-consuming, that even victims of Soviet repressions would sometimes appeal their sentences even after being released from the Gulag: Adler's research documents a set of Gulag survivors who sought reinstatement in the Party even after it had abused them by sending them to prison on false charges. They considered the time spent to be a penance for their supposed crimes, which they often convinced themselves they had committed due to their absolute faith in the Party. Historian Nanci Adler investigates this mass Stockholm syndrome in her book *Keeping Faith with the Party*, in which she profiles several such cases of misplaced guilt and self-flagellation over invented crimes.[10]

The great irony of communism is that it always fails to deliver on its own materialistic promises. As we know, all worldly goods will pass away. They are necessarily ephemeral. To replace the eternal things of God with even the most beautiful of earthly things is pure folly. Yet the entire communist system is founded on this tradeoff.

[10] Nanci Adler, *Keeping Faith with the Party: Communist Believers Return from the Gulag* (Bloomington, IN: Indiana University Press, 2012).

CHAPTER TWO

Cuba

Havana, 1961: The Poison Apple

"Close your eyes! Hold out your hands!"

Confused schoolchildren obediently did as their teachers instructed.

"Ask God for a piece of candy."

The seconds ticked by as the candy, inevitably, did not materialize.

"Now ask *Fidel* for a piece of candy."

With that, the communist teachers made their way around the room, distributing candy poisoned with their utopian ideology.

This Pavlovian scene repeated itself in schoolrooms across Cuba in the years after the takeover by Fidel Castro's regime. Castro, who initially lied about the nature of his regime following the hoped-for 1959 revolution, promised that "the Revolution is as green as palm trees!" As Cubans would soon learn, his promises, like that of the free candy, were all false.

As the dystopian candy routine illustrates, the propagandizing began early—both in the regime's first months and in the lives of the students.

As always, communists operate under layers of concealment, to maintain plausible deniability in misdirecting the public away from their true aims. One tactic that the Castro regime undertook in this vein was an allocation of resources to what became a remarkably successful literacy campaign. No time was wasted: In 1961, legions of enthusiastic "brigadistas" were dispatched to all corners of Cuba to deliver not only the ability to read and write, but also a sense of "solidarity" grounded in the new revolutionary ideology of brotherhood and equality. In just over a year, literacy rates skyrocketed from around 65 percent to nearly 100 percent.

Like the candy in the schoolroom, this gift of literacy was a poisoned apple. Communist ideals were taught along with the alphabet, and vocabulary was carefully selected to construct a worldview in line with Castro's utopian vision. The first words that 30 to 40 percent of the island's residents first committed to paper were propaganda.

The focus on literacy was a typical social engineering tool used in communist states. Many indigenous, spoken languages in the territories of the U.S.S.R. were written down for the first time under the widespread Soviet literacy projects. The seemingly noble goal of a literate, prosperous, free populace is the cloak under which communism conceals its more nefarious purposes. There may be great strides in human achievement, at least at the beginning. But at what cost?

✠ ✠ ✠

As a country with imperial Spanish roots, Cuba is historically Catholic, characterized by deep religious devotion and its indelible imprints on the culture. Once a "ringing island" like England was, Cuba was a Catholic stronghold, a global pilgrimage destination, and a fertile ground for religious communities.

Before the Revolution

Particularly strong, even throughout the days of Castro, were the country's Catholic schools. Two in particular, Belen (Spanish for "Bethlehem") and La Salle (named after St. John Baptiste de La

Salle), were staffed by Jesuits and Christian Brothers, respectively. The Castro brothers themselves attended Belen. But so did the counterrevolutionaries. Secularization of the schools began in the 1920s, but, as we will see, some strong Catholic sentiment remained despite the Modernist "soft" revolution.

In the communist narrative, Catholicism — or, more specifically, the institution of the Roman Catholic Church — was associated with Western capitalist power structures. In a theme that we will see repeated, religious and political persecution intertwined as much as the anti-Catholicism and anti-capitalism of the regime overlapped. Likewise, the motivations of dissenters, counterrevolutionaries, and freedom fighters contained both religious and political elements, often indistinguishable in practice.

Even during the Cuban independence movement, Cubans grappled with the political connotations of their Catholic identity. The Church was deeply associated with the Spanish Empire, which had brought the Faith to the island. Therefore, devotion to the Church was, in some revolutionary corners, considered a potential threat to Cuban independence. The nation survived this era of conflicted Catholic identity and remained a strong bulwark of the Faith from the time of independence, synthesizing devoted loyalty to the Church with a fierce national pride. Thus, the rallying cry of "*Dios, Patria, y Vida*" (God, Homeland, and Life) has been on the lips of Cuban patriots throughout the trials of communism, right through the contemporary demonstrations against the totalitarian government in the summer of 2021.

1962: The Repressions Begin

As always, communist regimes create a political pretext to persecute the Church. In addition to its inherent crime against state-atheism, the Church was accused of being a fifth column, a counterrevolutionary force representing bourgeois foreign interests. The historical perception of the Church as primarily an imperial Spanish institution didn't help assuage these fears.

In 1962, Castro suppressed the clergy, shutting down monasteries, expelling priests, and nationalizing Church property. He also began a campaign of blackmail and coercion against the clergy, inducing many to collaborate with the junta government rather than face deportation. Some clergy justified their collaboration, claiming that the ends justified the means. Otherwise, where would the Church be?

The Accusation of the Conscience

For some Cuban Catholics, simply avoiding outright persecution was not enough. As Bay of Pigs veteran Ricardo Sanchez says, "What's the point of believing something if you're not going to act?"

Leopoldo "Polo" Aguilera is one such Catholic, whose deep faith and patriotism drove him to take brave, decisive action.

Polo grew up in an affluent family marked by tragedy. His parents divorced when he was young, and the family had an indifferent attitude toward the Faith. Like many Cuban Catholics, Polo attended Catholic school. He recalls that he never really connected with his faith until a formative experience with a pious priest at La Salle, a leading preparatory school. After exams, the teachers hosted a giveaway with a series of prizes for academic achievement. Polo spotted a crucifix among a priest's belongings, not on the prize table.

"I had to have it," he remembers. The priest, sensing the great graces this young soul would gain from the sacramental item, generously gave over the crucifix. It was at that moment that Polo truly started to study the Faith and grow in prayer and virtue.

This very same crucifix now adorns Polo's office—which doubles as a shrine of sorts to Cuban freedom fighters, replete with an archive of newspaper clippings, photographs, and books—in his Miami home. It has been with him for decades, from his life under communism to his escape from Cuba, through his marriage and family life, to his present retired life in Miami as an active Catholic, researcher, and proud member of the Bay of Pigs Museum. To this day, Polo still travels everywhere with the crucifix, including on international flights!

Polo was a young man when the revolution began. He had been assisting his father on his rice and cattle farm on the southern coast of Cuba, learning the family business. After marrying, he lived with his wife, father, brother, and sister-in-law on the family's farm.

Polo holds his crucifix near a wall of his office
dedicated to the Cuban freedom fighters.

Polo Aguilera and the author in Polo's extensive office

Polo awoke one day to the sound of trucks rolling through his fields. He looked outside to see soldiers crawling around the crops, then banging on the door.

Polo ran outside to see what the commotion was about. It was then that he saw Che Guevara himself strolling through the rice fields. Che's men began loading the Aguilera family's property, including bushels of their cash crop of rice, onto the trucks.

Che smooth-talked Polo's father: the state must confiscate your property out of necessity, but don't worry! We will reimburse you in government bonds. Polo didn't believe him for a second.

At that point, the family realized their future in Cuba was at risk. Sensing the coming tide, they made the decision to move to Miami. Frantically, they had to quickly pack up everything they owned and escape the island before it was too late.

Polo had only $700 in cash. He deftly hid it in his cigarette case. He remembers feeling lucky that the soldiers who searched them didn't smoke!

When he landed in Miami, he was just able to rent a Coral Gables apartment. With only $600 left to his name, he was forced to build his life back up from scratch.

Polo had never been involved in politics. But he couldn't walk away now. His livelihood, his homeland, and his faith were now at stake. He began casting about for anti-communist groups to get involved with in Miami. He met with a few of them, searching until he found the right fit. Polo remembers being disillusioned by some of the groups, who were populated with men who had been fervent supporters of Fidel Castro just months earlier. Polo was sympathetic to their plight—he knew many had been fooled by Fidel. But with the layers of intrigue, and his family's safety on the line, he wasn't sure he could trust such changeable men.

One day, Polo came upon his old football coach from Havana who, by chance, was now also in Miami. They got to talking. The coach revealed that he was now working with the CIA. Their mission was to smuggle weapons into Cuba to supply the underground rebel army. "You'll get to be a commando!" the coach joked.

Polo immediately signed up. This was the opportunity he had been waiting for! He no longer had to remain helpless as his country was dismantled.

He embarked for training in the Florida Keys. He was paired with a group of other Cuban exiles, and assigned a large but slow forty-foot boat. They practiced their maneuvers in the Florida waters, preparing for the roughly ninety-mile journey to Havana. For the first time, Polo learned to shoot a machine gun.

In January 1961, the group was sent on its first expeditionary mission. The team loaded the boat with weapons and set off for Havana. They knew that stealth was essential: with a top speed of twenty miles per hour, the vessel would not be fast enough to outrun the Cuban navy.

The team was equipped with three machine guns, but there was only one belt of ammunition per gun. They would have to make it last.

The CIA contact had made their simple mission clear: they were to pull into the bay at the eastern side of Havana. Another CIA agent would be on the other side. When the signal was given, they would transfer the weapons to him, then head back home.

The little boat pulled into the Bay of Havana right on time, waiting at the appointed spot. No one was there. Getting nervous, they called the CIA agent. There was no response. Knowing that each minute there risked more undue attention, they turned around and headed back for Florida.

On mission number two, the winter sea was roiling so badly that one of the men got seasick. Nevertheless, the craft pushed forward to the agreed-upon location. Nothing again. No answer. Back to Florida they went.

On the third attempt, it took eight hours to get to Havana, this time at night. Halfway through the trip, they noticed lights behind them and thought they were being chased. Picking up the guns, they lit up the boat's mast, as was required. One of the men wanted to fire, but the others talked him down. This was a providential move, as the other vessel turned out to be one of theirs. The second craft, full of freedom fighters on a similar weapons-smuggling mission, passed them silently in the night.

The fourth trip was the most dramatic. They embarked on the roughest seas they had yet seen. Already taking on water because of the weather, the boat was in rough shape. It was at that point that the crew heard an explosion. Rushing to the front, they couldn't believe their eyes. The boat had collided with a whale! The impact destroyed the front of the boat—along with all their electronics and communication equipment. Without any way to reach their contacts, and with the boat rapidly taking on water, they returned yet again to Florida.

The fifth and final mission occurred just two days before the Bay of Pigs Invasion. It was imperative that these weapons be delivered this time—this was the final chance. Instead of Havana, the CIA agent directed them to a smaller bay in a more central location on the island, reflecting President John F. Kennedy's last-minute changes to the invasion plans.

Polo remembers that this trip was the only time the group had a flat ocean. It was the calm before the storm.

Halfway through the journey, the comms equipment started beeping. It was their CIA contact. "Turn around!" he said, warning the crew that the Cuban navy was patrolling at their destination heavily. It could be a suicide mission.

Polo and his companions had a different reaction. "Good!" they thought. After all these months of waiting, maybe now they'd have the chance to actually engage with the enemy. They were desperate for any sort of dent in the gridlock. By the time they pulled up to the designated harbor, there were no naval vessels to be seen.

Unsurprisingly by this time, no CIA contacts were waiting on the other side. Against the odds, the team called their agent to let him know they had made it. He didn't respond. In a final effort, they camped out overnight in the boat, staying from the afternoon through six o'clock the next morning. This was undoubtedly a risky move in a dangerous dance where every move was highly choreographed.

In the end, they pulled up the chain from a buoy at the entrance to the harbor and tied all the packages of weapons securely in place. Hopefully *someone* would find them. After four failed attempts, this was a last-ditch effort. Calling the agent one last time, they explained where the packages were, telling him they wouldn't be making any more of these frustrating, fruitless missions. Two days later, the ill-fated Bay of Pigs Invasion plunged the Cuban resistance forces into a full-scale operation. Polo doesn't know if the weapons were ever found.

Polo remains proud of his actions in the resistance, but when he looks back he feels deeply betrayed by the flimsy promises and disorganization of the CIA. "It was all a scam," he says. In a pattern that would be fully realized in the invasion itself, the passionate resistance of the Cuban exiles had been rendered practically ineffectual by these strategic blunders.

The CIA's treatment of Cuban assets has long been a subject of controversy. The agency's inability to commit to a plan in Cuba resulted in lost connections, miscommunication, and, sometimes, total abandonment. This pattern would come to a head dramatically at the Bay of Pigs, which we will cover later in this chapter. The cavalier attitude of the CIA, which always sought to maintain plausible deniability of its Cuban operations, meant that these men were taking greater risks than they ever agreed to.

Polo recalls another incident that made him wonder about the layers of deception and infiltration in the anti-communist circles.

While training in the Florida Keys for the smuggling missions, a small platoon of uncertain allegiance came blustering into the camp. Their leader harassed Polo, pointing his gun and demanding that he tell them how to get off the island. Polo had no idea what they wanted. But then the answer was, literally, illuminated for him. "It had to be God," he says. The moonlight suddenly revealed a small boat in the lagoon. Polo seized the opportunity, pointing it out to the furious junta. The soldiers boarded and revved full speed ahead, directly into a sandbar. Whatever their intent that evening, it was thwarted.

Months later, back in Miami, Polo was invited to a movie screening with the John Birch Society, a well-known anti-communist league. Among the members, Polo spotted the same man who had pointed the gun at him that night on the Keys. What was he doing here?

This confusion and distrust is the legacy of communism. Polo characterizes communism in three words: "Division, division, division."

I asked Polo why he could see through Castro's lies when others were fooled. He traces it all back to that formative moment when Che Guevara stole his property right in front of him, all the while spouting euphemisms. He had also heard of friends and acquaintances being executed by the glorious new regime. "I didn't need anything more than that."

When asked why he risked his life and property, Polo responds as though the answer is a given: "I couldn't stand by and watch this happen to my country."

As Catholics know, there are sins of commission and sins of omission. The accusation of the conscience would be more painful than any punishment levied by man.

If Polo and his compatriots had been caught, they could have been sentenced to up to thirty years in political prison. Thirty years was the maximum penal sentence. Any "crime" worse than a thirty-year sentence merited instant execution. Had he been caught, he would have been plunged into the island's vast ecosystem of prison camps. It is there that we go next.

✠ ✠ ✠

Arturo León Carrazana was born in July of 1935, in a rural neighborhood of the city of Santa Clara, in the ancient province of Las Villas. Born to a hardworking agrarian family, he was the eighth of nine brothers. He remembers the simplicity of rural life: kept busy by the hard seasons of work, the family did not have much time for formal religious instruction, but his parents made sure each of their children was baptized. Like many Cubans, the family had a devotion to the *Virgen del Cobre*, and also kept a rigorous Holy Week, as their fathers had before them.

Arturo recalls, "When Fidel came with his revolution, he did not catch me unprepared." He credits early education on the true nature of communism as an ideological inoculation that would protect him from the communists' aggressive propaganda years later.

Due to the influence of a staunchly anti-communist neighbor, Arturo had come to learn, at a young age, about the horrors of communism being played out across Eastern Europe. When he was eleven or twelve years old, Arturo would run to his neighbor's farm to borrow the latest issue of selections from *Reader's Digest*, originally printed in the United States and available in translation. Communist atrocities stained every page: the Soviet massacre of Polish soldiers at Katyn Forest, the repressions in East Germany, and the persecution of the clergy in Hungary. Stunned, Arturo read on. He learned from these pages that communists hated Christianity. He also learned that communists lie. The Katyn Forest Massacre, committed by Soviet soldiers in April and May of 1940, involved the death of some twenty-two thousand Polish officers who were being held as prisoners of war. The Soviet Union, refusing to lose face with its allies during the war, pinned blame on the Nazis, a story they stuck with until the 1990s, when overwhelming evidence forced Premier Mikhail Gorbachev to admit to the Soviet crime. This information left a lasting impression on the young boy. Communism, then just a barbaric ideology in a distant land, was defined by hostility toward God, brutality, and deceit.

And then the scourge of communism came to Cuba. When Fidel came to power, Arturo started to recognize some of these signs that he had observed in the pages of *Reader's Digest*.

Fidel was certainly brutal, and he acted against God, expelling priests whom he considered to be ideological enemies. In addition, Fidel lied. He promised that his revolution was "as green as palm trees," obfuscating his communist ideology. He spoke out of both sides of his mouth.

All the hallmarks were there. Could what had happened in Russia and so many other places really repeat itself here in Cuba?

Arturo is grateful for his early years of "anticommunist instruction," gained in astute reading, observation, and discernment. He was immune to the brainwashing that infected many of his countrymen, whose blind fanaticism toward Fidel was rooted in a naive belief in his false promises.

One of Fidel Castro's first sweeping actions in office was to repress Catholic clergy.

From 1959 to 1962, Fidel expelled hundreds of priests from the island. Denigrating the Church as the "fifth column of the counter-revolution," Fidel especially targeted the clergy as purported Vatican spies. Some of these priests would end up in Miami, where they and other expats ministered to the Cuban diaspora. Several would later be involved in the Bay of Pigs Invasion. Fidel's measures were swift and merciless: over the course of one day, 131 priests were deported on a freight ship set for Spain.

Fidel and his brother Raul, who succeeded him as dictator of Cuba, were given a strong Catholic upbringing and Jesuit education. After being kicked out of the La Salle boarding school in Santiago, Fidel transferred to Belen Preparatory School—as we noted earlier, one of the premier Catholic high schools in Cuba. In addition to having rigorous academics, the college identified strongly with Catholic Action—the true Catholic Action instituted by Pius IX, which flourished throughout the 1920s and beyond. Ironically, this Catholic Action became a strong bastion of resistance against the injustices of Fidel's regime. Despite his early foundation, the religious education did not stick with Fidel, as he began to get involved in politics and became enamored with Marxism.

Fidel Castro's relationship to the Catholic Church is a difficult, convoluted, and often contradictory one. His initial outright hatred transmogrified into a kind of halfway apostasy, in which he claimed membership in the Church while trying to subvert her doctrines to fit communism. He was thus a great admirer of the Catholic-flavored variety of Marxism known as liberation theology.

In a book-length interview with a liberation theologian named Frei Betto, *Fidel y la Religion,* Fidel expounded on his philosophy. At times, he demonstrates a clear understanding of Catholic principles:

> I think all of the Church's martyrs were impelled by feelings
> of loyalty, because they believed strongly in something.
> The idea of the hereafter, where their actions would merit
> reward, might have been of some help, but I don't think
> it was the main reason. People who do something out of

fear generally fear the fire, the martyrdom, and the torture even more. They don't dare to defy them. People who are concerned about obtaining material possessions, pleasure, or rewards try to save their lives, not sacrifice them. I think that throughout the Church's history its martyrs must have been motivated by something more inspiring than fear or punishment. It's much easier for me to understand that.[11]

Yet he immediately reappropriates these Catholic principles for his own ends.

I've called for self-sacrifice and, at times, for martyrdom, heroism, and death. I think it's a great idea for a man to give his life for a revolutionary idea and to fight, knowing he may die. *Even though he knows there's nothing after death*, he upholds the idea, the moral value, so firmly that he defends it with everything he has—his life—without expecting reward or punishment.[12]

Castro is inspired by martyrs not because they upheld the Catholic Faith unto death, but because their heroism and dedication to a cause—any cause—provided a model for the type of devotion he expected from his communist followers. Fidel expects his devotees to die for him and become martyrs for his revolution in the way that Catholic martyrs die for God and eternal life. Fidel unwittingly shows here that he has replaced God with the communist utopian state. He then explicitly denies the immortality of the soul, a foundational Catholic teaching. At the center of this discourse is

[11] Frei Betto and Fidel Castro, *Fidel and Religion: Conversations with Frei Betto on Marxism and Liberation Theology* (North Melbourne, Australia: Ocean Press, 2006), 124–125.
[12] Ibid., 125.

Fidel's pride and thirst for power—his gospel is one of conflict and domination, not humility and accord.

Liberation theology proved to be a dangerous pseudo-Catholicism that led souls astray by cloaking atheist doctrine in Catholic concepts, words, and imagery. (The psychological warfare of liberation theology thus operated much in the same way that the National Church of Czechoslovakia did, as we will see in the next section.) Fidel's tactics of corrupting the teachings of the Catholic Church with false ideas served to muddy the waters, and to sow confusion about his own beliefs. While colored by his Catholic roots, his new, prideful religion was a faith all its own. Fidel sought to create a church in his own image, just like Henry VIII. Later in life, he would claim to be a Catholic, going through all the external motions while at the same time overseeing a murderous program of re-education, oppression, and subjugation. The performance of Catholicism, devoid of beliefs, virtue, or supernatural reality, seemed to characterize the dictator's "Christian faith."

Many Catholics saw through these advanced lies. Fidel's commentary on martyrs is ironic, considering that he was himself facilitating true martyrs' entry into the Kingdom of Heaven in the prison camps of his "glorious" revolution.

✠ ✠ ✠

At the time of the revolution, already a young man, Arturo was a member of the Marines, working at an office in Havana. Despite his position in the military, he could not in good conscience go along with Fidel's program.

In his daily life as a soldier, Arturo began to become disillusioned with the regime, as it tightened restrictions on civil and ecclesiastical life. He saw through Fidel's political sophistry and identified his latent communist ideas—Fidel's actions spoke louder than his words.

With his military perspective, Arturo noted Castro's cowardice: Fidel had come to be known as capitan araña—captain spider—since he would gladly send his followers to fight, but would himself hang back from danger. He began to get involved in counterrevolutionary activities. Finding a group of trustworthy compatriots proved a challenge. Arturo had to connect through friends who were well identified in their anti-communist beliefs. But there were always infiltrators in the anti-communist organizations. Infiltrators and informants infested all organizations, making it difficult to know who to trust.

After consolidating power, Fidel had quickly created the Committees of the Defense of the Revolution (CDR), a network of informers, utilized to watch out for and denounce to the intelligence service all activity contrary to the revolution. For adults, this meant that keeping your job was often contingent on enthusiastic membership in a Communist group such as the Revolutionary Militia, the CDR, the Federation of Cuban Women, and so on.

Students were expected to be members of the Union of Communist Youth (UJC, *Union de Jovenes Comunistas*). In order to have access to secondary education or to enter the universities, one had to be a member of some Communist institution. They would say: "One has to be clear." Unconscionable loyalty tests were demanded. If you were not well identified with the revolution, you could not enter higher education.

To navigate these waters, some turned to deception, employing the regime's own tools against it. The "two-faced," as Arturo refers to them, were made up of the youth who did not genuinely sympathize with the revolution but would feign a false sympathy for communist ideas and, in so doing, be able to enter higher education institutes.

At the universities themselves, the main subject was Marxism. Regardless of one's official major, if one did not pass that subject—a highly subjective ideological litmus test—one did not pass that grade level and therefore could not obtain any degree.

Due to this atmosphere of distrust and uncertainty, Arturo notes that many Cubans who felt called to resistance preferred to take renegade individual action rather than become entangled with a group. It may not have been as effective a strategy as organized resistance, but it was safer. Short of threats or torture, you would not inform on yourself. Arturo explains that this strategy is still employed today, as the culture of informing and infiltration still reigns supreme in Cuba.

✠ ✠ ✠

By 1962, several organized resistance groups had formed in Cuba, with various methodologies, goals, and core beliefs but with the same guiding star: Fidel and his revolution were evil and must be stopped. Often bolstered by American aid, these groups engaged in guerilla warfare and sabotage operations to weaken Fidel's junta army.

Arturo became involved with *Frente Anticomunista de Liberacion* (FAL). The group organized an uprising in 1962, as part of the ongoing guerilla warfare between Cuban freedom fighters and troops loyal to the Castro regime.

Some perished during the skirmish. The rest of the members who were caught were put into La Cabaña, an eighteenth-century Spanish fortress converted by Castro into a political prison. Arturo was captured and sentenced to thirty years in prison for counterrevolutionary activity.

A large number of Arturo's compatriots were executed in the days after the uprising.[13] From his holding cell, Arturo could hear the drama unfold. "I could hear the orders for the unloading of the shots of those executed," he recalls, "and their cries of 'Viva

---

[13] The freedom fighters killed in this way were colloquially referred to as *fusilados,* meaning executed by firing squad.

Cristo Rey,' in the pits of La Cabaña on the 19th, 20th, and 21st of September of 1962."

"Viva Cristo Rey!" (Long live Christ the King!) was a perennial refrain that reverberated along the prison walls.

✠ ✠ ✠

Arturo would go on to spend a total of seventeen years in the political prison system. He was released due to negotiations with President Jimmy Carter.

His survived untold deprivation, injustice, and human rights abuses. From La Cabaña he was taken to Isla de Pinos.[14] There, he underwent the so-called *Plan de Trabajo Forzado Camilo Cienfuegos*, a program of forced labor. The forced labor program, so characteristic of sufferings in concentration camps across the globe, was an attempt by the regime to make use of the enemies of the revolution.

The men would return from long, hot days of backbreaking work to spare accommodations and empty plates. Their sores, wounds, and illnesses would go untreated: due to the embargo, the regime could barely afford sufficient medical supplies for the general population, never mind enemies of the state.

The inmates also experienced extremely high psychological pressure. The communist guards used sly tactics to induce intellectual surrender, apostasy, or submission. Arturo faced a particularly crafty campaign.

The inmates were all given the option of "re-education." They would undergo classes, training, and exercises, eventually renouncing their counterrevolutionary activities; sometimes even renouncing their Christian faith. They would be subjected to Marxist

---

[14] The island is today called Isla de la Juventud (Isle of Youth) by the regime.

indoctrination, day in and day out, brainwashed into good and loyal comrades.

In exchange, they would first be given perks within the camp: better rations, more comfortable sleeping quarters, more sanitary cells, increased access to the outside world, the ability to correspond with their families. Eventually, if they behaved and showed the requisite loyalty, they might be released.

Some prisoners, made desperate by the hunger, work, and hellish conditions, leaped at the opportunity. Arturo estimates that up to 70 percent of political prisoners opted for re-education of some kind. The other 30 percent refused. Among them was Arturo. He would not sell his soul.

Those prisoners who refused re-education were known as *plantados*, meaning that they were planted firmly in their beliefs. The name was first used in 1964, after three prisoners refused forced labor.[15] The immovable *plantados* were made to wear yellow uniforms to distinguish them from the rest of the inmates, who wore blue. Other prisoners looked upon them with an awed respect, while the guards regarded them with increased sadism and fury.

The regime didn't know what to do with them. They had already demonstrated they were not so gullible or venal. They were also the prisoners most likely to go on hunger strikes. Such strength intimidated the guards, who were used to ruling through intimidation. So they resorted to torture.

The *plantados* were isolated, publicly humiliated, and subjected to all manner of brutalization. A comprehensive archive of testimonies about the *plantados* can be found at Losplantados.com.

---

[15] See the website for Plantado (Plantados Project): https://losplantados. com/plantados-project-2/.

Years later, Arturo connected with a friend who had suffered unspeakable tortures as a *plantado* in another camp. He had never fully physically recovered. But he lived. His survival was an act of resistance. Arturo is grateful to God that he was spared the worst of these tortures. But the guards' psychological abuse was more nefarious than even the worst physical pain.

✠ ✠ ✠

Soul Killing in the Prisons

> *"Communism tries to steal your property. That's okay, we*
> *can handle that. But it tries to steal your soul…"*
> — A Cuban expat

Prison guards played myriad psychological games to induce mental and spiritual surrender. The most nefarious of these schemes, also used by the communists during the Spanish Civil War, makes explicit the communist hatred of a soul in the state of grace.

Guards would bribe a prisoner, promising him luxuries, comfort, rations, and freedom if he would consent to be re-educated. This would mark a political victory. But, filled with hatred at the backwards ideology that limited the progress of the revolution, guards would also try to induce apostasy from the Faith. Despite their professed atheism, these communists, like Satan, sought the damnation of souls.

With forked tongues, they crooned, "It's okay, it's just a word. Renounce the Faith now, you don't have to mean it. You can always go to Confession when you're released."

It is the challenge posed to martyrs of every century, from the grain of incense demanded of Roman martyrs to the one toe stepping on the icons of the Christians of Japan.

Many Catholics knew to resist this lie of their captors.

But every so often, a prisoner, desperate from starvation and abuse, would believe it. The ramifications of this action rushed through the prisoner's mind: *So what if I say what I have to say? This guard just wants a show, he wants to feel powerful. I'll play the game, then I will be released. I can go straight to Confession, then live out my days with my family! And go to Mass every week! Really, this would be better for my soul in the long run.*

Talking himself into it, the defeated prisoner weakly, guiltily recited a renunciation of Faith.

Almost over. Just a few more steps, some more red tape, a few more days of maggot-infested rations, and then he'd be free.

No sooner had the words left his mouth than the guard screeched with delight.

"Ha! You denied your God! Where is He now?"

Fear.

Cocking his pistol, the guard continued the abuse.

"You believed me! How's that for faith?"

Aiming at the prisoner's skull, the guard demonically rejoiced: "You're still going to die—but now you're going to Hell."

The shot fired.

Forgive them, Lord, for they know not what they do.

✠ ✠ ✠

Under these circumstances, faith is pushed to the limit.

One of the most notable of the *plantados* is Armando Valladares, a prisoner of conscience who had initially been arrested and sentenced to thirty years simply for refusing to proudly display an "I'm with Fidel" placard on his desk at his government job. He suffered years in the prisons of Cuba, refusing the offer of "rehabilitation." He spent time at both the La Cabaña and Isla des Pinos prisons where Arturo León was incarcerated.

After Valladares's release, he went on to write his experiences in the moving memoir *Against All Hope: A Memoir of Life in Castro's Gulag*. Valladares became a public speaker, a human rights advocate, and eventually an ambassador to the United Nations. His work played a pivotal role in raising global awareness about the horrors of Castro's Cuba at a time when this information was heavily repressed by the regime. Among the atrocities described in Valladares's memoirs are sleep deprivation, starvation, beatings, sadistic torture, and even biological experimentation after the fashion of the notorious Nazi Dr. Mengele, pushing the limits on prisoners' malnourished bodies.

After the physical and psychological toll of the camps, Valladares appealed to Heaven: "I sought God then. My conversations with him brought me a spiritual strength to bear up under these conditions.... without sickening with hatred. I only prayed for Him to accompany me. And His presence, which I felt, made my faith an indestructible shield."[16]

The same was true for Arturo León. He notes, "My belief in God always maintained in me faith and hope." His status as a *plantado* meant that he was witness to some of the worst abuses in the camps, but he was also witness to some of its most poignant miracles.

One of these miracles occurred on Fridays on the open-air sixth floor of one of the "circulars."

Arturo explains the layout of the prison. Isla de Pinos consisted of four circular buildings of six floors each. The sixth floor was more of an open floor plan, without walls and individual cells. Here, Catholic prisoners would gather together to attend Mass. Priests were

---

[16] Armando Valladares, *Against All Hope: A Memoir of Life in Castro's Gulag*, trans. Andrew Hurley (New York: Encounter Books, 2001), 151.

incarcerated only in the first circular. When possible, they would say Mass for the prisoners, confect and consume the Eucharist. In the other three circulars, this great grace was impossible. Instead of wallowing in self-pity, these prisoners decided they would pray all the prayers of the Mass anyway. In the absence of priests, they recited the prayers from memory. When they got to the canon, they reverently bowed their heads at the point when the consecration would normally occur, making fervent spiritual communions.

The prisoners' ability to gather for Catholic prayer in an environment where possessing a Bible was itself a major crime is nothing short of providential.

✠ ✠ ✠

Arturo gained his freedom on October 13, 1979, after seventeen years in prison.

After his ordeal in Isla de Pinos, he was moved to another prison, Sandino Number 3. He was then shuffled to Arisa, and then to Boniato. The network of Cuban gulags was almost as complex an organ as the Soviet archipelago. He was again moved to Manacas in 1970, and finally to Nieves Morejón in 1974, where he stayed until his release.

Arturo's release in 1979 was part of President Jimmy Carter's ongoing negotiations with the Castro regime, which, aided by the involvement of Cuban exiles, emphasized the human rights component over nuclear or economic policy. Free for the first time in almost two decades, Arturo spent the next several months reacclimating to life in Cuba proper.

Much had changed, but much had stayed the same. Because of the embargo and Castro's disastrous economic policies, Cuba was (and remains) a time capsule. For many released prisoners, facing the sad realities of Castro's Cuba upon release was very discouraging.

The prison had been a microcosm of the poverty and repression that plagued the entire island.

As part of his amnesty, Arturo was given the opportunity to emigrate to the United States. On January 24, 1980, he boarded a plane set for Miami and its glittering future.

Despite the tribulations of his early adulthood, Arturo made a home in Miami, eventually married, and had a family. He has assimilated his experiences under communist oppression, emerging victorious: "I do not consider myself 'a victim of communism.' I consider myself a fighter for reason and for democracy, and for the Faith."

Arturo remains immensely grateful for his American citizenship and the opportunities it affords. He and his son are eager to tell his story to honor his life and warn future generations of the evils of communism. Despite our nation's commitment to liberty, many Americans remain ignorant of communism's death toll, sporting Che Guevara t-shirts with little consideration for his victims. Arturo observes:

> Here in the United States, there is much ignorance about
> Marxist ideology, of how it is disguised with a populist
> language of social justice that is never carried out. Gen-
> der ideology, which they carry out with unnatural sexual
> education given to children, along with the changes they
> want to carry out with the New World Order, is all part
> of the communist doctrine based on neo-Marxism. None
> of these will be able to triumph.

Communism has oppressed Cuba for sixty-four years, quickly approaching the Soviet Union's lifespan of seventy-four years.[17] Conditions for Cuban citizens remain dire, despite Potemkin political

---

[17] It is sixty-nine years if you start counting from the formal establishment of the USSR in 1922, rather than from the date of the revolution in 1917.

tours organized by communist authorities to fool wanderlusting Westerners. And, despite numerous papal visits, the government's plan for the Church's future remains uncertain.

In spite of the two-thirds of a century gridlock, Arturo remains hopeful for the fate of his homeland. "Today Cuba is a hell of hunger and physical needs and of official atheism. We are strong because Christ is the foundation of our struggle. So, in the end, we'll triumph, and Cuba will once again be free and Christian. The gates of hell shall not prevail."

The Martyrs of the MRR

Cuban resistance largely centered around the training of an invasion force, which conducted guerilla warfare against Castro's troops, and which ultimately culminated in the Bay of Pigs Invasion of April 17–20, 1961. This army of exiles was based in Florida and was trained directly by the CIA in Guatemala, Puerto Rico, Nicaragua, and Panama.

It was composed of particularly devoted and idealistic men. Victor Triay, historian of Cuba and visiting fellow at the Brigade 2506 Museum in Miami, states that religious motivation was central to the freedom fighters' mission. "They were inseparable," he insists. The main players in these groups were well known for their Catholic devotion, which in turn spurred their zeal to defend their homeland from the injustices of the communist regime.

Countering the damage wrought by their apostate alumni, the Jesuit and Christian Brothers preparatory schools Belen and La Salle became hotbeds of resistance to the Castro regime. Their students had taken up the Vatican's exhortation to Catholic Action since Pius IX's first exhortation. Now, the time had come to put faith into action.

In addition to preserving the Faith, which was existentially threatened by Castro's policies, these martyrs of Cuba understood the importance of the social kingship of Christ. Since the 1920s, when the mounting secularization of Cuba threatened to remove Christ from the public sphere, the Catholic Action movements took on Pius X's mission "to restore all things in Christ." In the face of the communist revolution, they adapted their methods, taking seriously the obligation to bring Christ into the public sphere, and to honor Him in their defiance of totalitarian usurpers.

Thus, as the *Cristeros* had in Mexico at the beginning of the century, the Cubans' exaltation of Christ the King signified that they would not submit to false authority. The atheist-communist regime had seized its power unlawfully, as the only true authority came from God. Christ was not to be sequestered away in private worship, to be ignored when challenged by hostile leaders. He was King of the Universe, and they would act accordingly. The Faith was not something to be kept out of politics — it was something that guided all political and social participation. So when the Faith became illegal, living the Faith became a matter of political resistance.

Thus the martyrs' refrain of *Viva Cristo Rey* signified not only the promise of the Kingdom of Heaven, but also the building of that Kingdom here on earth.

Student Julio Bordas created the Movement of Revolutionary Recovery (MMR), an anti-Castro organization that sought to rescue the revolution from the communist hijacking and restore it to its rightful trajectory.

Uniting forces with the MRR was the *Agrupacion Catolica Universitaria*, a student Catholic Action organization whose members, *Agruppados*, were already active in defending the Faith on campus. Many of these men would lose their lives in combat or in the prisons. One of the foremost members of the MRR, Manuel Artime, an idealistic leader of *Agrupacion* who helped form the stated mission of the MRR, expressed the organization's goals in its written "Body of Ideas." Artime wrote that the MRR's objective was "not only to overthrow Fidel Castro, but to permanently fight for an ideology of Christ, and for a reality of liberating our nation treacherously sold to the Communist International."[18] Expressions such as these lead Victor Triay to attest that the anti-communist movement had a "profound religious component."[19]

¡*Viva Cristo Rey!*

They are known, simply, as "our martyrs." Figures little-known outside of Cuban communities, these men merit recognition and emulation from all Catholics.

As is so often the case in situations of resistance to tyranny, the line between political and religious persecution is blurred. In the face of injustice, the Catholic Faith all but requires heroic resistance. Through a series of interviews, I probed into the motivations of the freedom fighters, attempting to define this line more clearly. What I discovered was that their faith and patriotism were almost indistinguishable. The Faith necessitated that they protect their freedoms, the rights of the Church, and the country to which they owed filial piety. The correctly ordered battle cry—*Dios, Patria, y Vida*—explains this: these priorities all flowed from the dedication to God. To the members of the MRR, resistance became an integral part of how they lived out their faith.

None of us can control the circumstances in which we are born. In some eras, it is easy to be a Catholic, even by worldly standards.

---

[18] Victor Triay, *Bay of Pigs: An Oral History of Brigade 2506* (Gainesville: University Press of Florida, 2001), 15. See footnote 32.

[19] Ibid.

In others, it is literally illegal. To live the Catholic life in such a situation is to confound worldly standards on a daily basis.

Extending to ancient times, martyrs have often been condemned officially for political reasons. To refuse to worship Caesar as a god, for example, earned a charge of treason under the Roman Empire. Our Lord Himself, in addition to the inconceivably false religious charges of blasphemy from the religious leaders of the Sanhedrin, was also accused of political crimes against the Roman Empire. The Canticle of the Three Young Men recounts the attempted martyrdom of the faithful Israelites who refused to appease Nebuchadnezzar's idolatry.

These brave Cuban men were martyrs for their cause, certainly. Martyrs for their homeland, definitely. They believed that freedom and justice were worth dying for.

But there is a strong case to be made that they are martyrs for the Church as well.

✠ ✠ ✠

Francisco

Rogelio González Corzo, code name "Francisco," was a leader of the MRR.

The youngest of three brothers, he was raised by hardworking parents in a simple, pious Catholic home. Educated at Belen, he had been notably devout and studious—a daily communicant, a good student, and an engaged citizen. He kept himself apprised of global news. His knowledge of the atrocities of the Spanish Civil War primed Rogelio to recognize and resist the same cacophony of horrors when they arose in his own homeland. The Spanish Civil War provided many instructive cases in Catholic resistance. Especially edifying were the Turon Martyrs, a group of eight Christian Brothers killed by insurrectionists in October 1934.

Rogelio knew of these atrocities but, far from discouraging him, he took inspiration from the strength of the martyrs and the supreme value of a religion that, refusing to be stamped out in the face of such persecution, could only be Truth. One can imagine that this knowledge helped fortify him throughout his perseverance in prison and courage unto death.

Rogelio used his Belen connections to build up the MRR, comprised of ready and willing patriots, mostly Catholic. He went on to command a total of seven thousand anti-Castro fighters in Cuba's Escambray Mountains, launching offensives against regime soldiers and laying the groundwork for an uprising or invasion. His resistance actions soon attracted the attention of the CIA, and he embarked on the first of several training missions, traveling secretly back and forth to Miami to prepare for the final battle.

Rogelio managed to evade capture for months, Cuban intelligence hot on his heels. He was eventually captured in March of 1961. He would be executed a mere thirty-three days after his capture. His fiancée, Dulce Carrera Justiz, had had to speak to him through coded telephone calls, and saw him only in secret, in a safehouse. Their final goodbye was through a coded phone call.[20] Dulce saw Rogelio's face one last time as the military convoy transporting him to La Cabaña passed by her house.[21]

Meanwhile, on April 17, the Bay of Pigs Invasion had begun. Fearing the anticipated popular uprising, the Castro government moved to quickly execute several leaders of the domestic resistance. Rogelio was brought before a communist court in La Cabaña prison for a two-day show trial. After the farce was over, he and several companions were sentenced to death by firing squad.

---

[20] Ann Ball, *Faces of Holiness: Modern Saints in Photos and Words*, vol. 1 (Huntingdon, IN: Our Sunday Visitor, 1998).

[21] Triay, *Bay of Pigs*, 176.

They were allowed to remain together in a cell, called the "chapel," praying together and encouraging each other in final perseverance. Before going before the firing squad, each of the men pledged to exclaim, "¡Viva Christo Rey! ¡Viva Cuba libre! ¡Viva el Directario Revolutionario Estudiantil!" (Long live Christ the King! Long live free Cuba! Long live the Revolutionary Student Directorate!) The freedom fighters pledged themselves, in order of importance, to Our Lord Jesus Christ, to a free Cuba, and to the MRR, the group that had sustained their active resistance.

Not all of the men were able to complete the entire battle cry. Rogelio's final *Viva* was silenced by the bullets.

His final written testament reveals his deep sense of duty to God and country:

> Dear parents and siblings:
>
> I know what the moment you receive the news of my death represents for you while you are far from where I am. I want to tell you that this was always what I asked God for. I think it would have been a greater moral and perhaps physical suffering for you if you had been here and had to go through all this time that lasted 32 days between my imprisonment and my death.
>
> Do not at any time be ashamed of my imprisonment and execution; on the contrary, I hope you are proud of your son and that you know how to adopt a correct position at the moment when God and the Fatherland asked for the sacrifice of your son. I want you to know that it was the only position I could have in situations like the one the country is going through right now.
>
> I am writing this at 2 am on April 20. I am in a cell that is called a chapel, since my death is a matter of minutes. I

want you to know in this way that my last thought on earth was for you and my dear brothers. Parents, brothers, I only have one terrible concern, but I am confident that, being my last will, this concern will cease to be so and will become a great joy: it is your spiritual life, your religious life. You know that to be a good Catholic and to obey God's will has always been of great importance to me. Right now I am sure that I am conducting myself in the way that God wants, and I wish that my death, of which you should be proud, serves the purpose of making you two, Mom and Dad, promise me that you will attend Mass every Sunday, go to Confession, receive Holy Communion, and do so regularly. That my brothers Manolito and Isidro make spiritual exercises, annually, that they confess and receive Communion monthly and go to Mass every Sunday. Try to be good spouses with these two jewels that you have, Laurita and Fifi, to whom I also ask you to improve your spiritual life. For my nephew Carlos Manuel to tell him how much his uncle loved him, that he died so that he would have a dignified and Catholic Cuba. And please send him to a Catholic school, because it is more important to save the soul than to learn English.

Many kisses for my godson and my two nieces. Send them too to Catholic schools, so that they may grow to be good sons and daughters. In these moments when death knocks on the door, you will know, parents and brothers, that I am very calm, the same as all my companions, since this opens the doors of heaven and eternal happiness for me. Also, it takes me next to my grandpa and my grandparents where, God willing, I wait for all of you. Remember, do not regret, this is for the best. Remember that I wait for you in Heaven, that you have strength as I have at this moment and that I leave with only one concern: for your spiritual life. Please, do not abandon it, that at no time will my problem affect your Catholicism, on the contrary, it will strengthen it. Without further ado, waiting for you in Heaven, your son remains, who never forgets you and waits for you with his grandparents,

Rogelio[22]

Rogelio's poetic and heartfelt letter proves him deeply Catholic, solicitous of the sacraments, and ever focused on the next life. He is painfully conscious of the suffering his death will cause his family, touchingly thinking of their needs instead of his own, even in his final moments. Yet despite the pain that his death brings, he emphasizes that this was the *only* course of action his conscience allowed in these circumstances.

He drives home the idea that good Catholics had no other option but to resist: "Do not at any time be ashamed of my imprisonment and execution; on the contrary, I hope you are proud of your son and that you know how to adopt a correct position at the moment when God and the Fatherland asked for the sacrifice of your son."

The proper conduct of a good Catholic is at the forefront of Rogelio's mind, in death as in life. His friends testify to his strong virtue from a young age. His final spiritual instructions to his family indicate a pattern of a devout life:

> You know that to be a good Catholic and to obey God's will has always been of great importance to me. Right now I am sure that I am conducting myself in the way that God wants, and I wish that my death, of which you should be

22 Letter of April 20, 1961, *Paralelo/24* 41 (April 1999), Hermanos al Rescate, http://www.hermanos.org/paralelo24/p24-41.html. Translated by the author.

proud, serves the purpose of making you two, Mom and Dad, promise me that you will attend Mass every Sunday, go to Confession, receive Holy Communion, and do so regularly.

Similarly, he is focused on the spiritual development and well-being of his nephew: "And please send him to a Catholic school, because it is more important to save the soul than to learn English. Many kisses for my godson and my two nieces. Send them too to Catholic schools, so that they may grow to be good sons and daughters."

Rogelio's resignation to his fate goes beyond simple acceptance: he believes that it is God's will that he die for God and country. He demonstrates a true understanding of the ancient maxim, "The blood of martyrs is the seed of the Church." And, with the peace that accompanies true sanctity, he hopes that his death will inspire his family to revitalize their spiritual life and to frequent the sacraments more fervently.

✠ ✠ ✠

Also executed that day was Alberto Tapia Ruano.

His final testament to his parents is equally devout and confident.

> Dear old folks [lit. *viejos*, a term of endearment],
>
> I just received the ratification of the Death Penalty a few moments ago and that is why, now that I am at the end, I am writing these lines to you. You will not believe me, but I can assure you that I have never had such peace of mind as at that moment: I sincerely feel very happy with the feeling that soon I will be with God, waiting and praying for you. Today at the trial I saw my brothers and godparents crying. Why's that? No and a thousand times No. I know that today is painful for you, but I want you to overcome yourselves and think that God in His infinite goodness has given me this grace to get right with Him, and everyone should give

Him thanks. Goodbye old folks, have much faith that in
Eternal Life I will intercede for all of you!

LONG LIVE CHRIST THE KING! Hugs and kisses,
no tears, everyone.

Goodbye brothers, godparents and family.

FAITH IN GOD.

Alberto[23]

Alberto's tranquil resignation to his fate and poignant meditation
on the Four Last Things exemplify a truly Catholic attitude in his
last moments.

In a wisdom gained by faith, he views the death penalty not as a
condemnation, but as a gift! How many people are given the grace
to know their hour of death, and therefore *prepare*? A provided death
is one of the greatest gifts a Catholic can receive. Despite the pitiful
circumstances, Alberto had eyes only for the next life.

Alberto's letter rises above the political ramifications of his imprisonment and death, refusing to let worldly matters, no matter how
significant, define his last moments. Untroubled by the accusations
of his supposed "crimes against the state," Alberto makes no attempt
to defend himself, knowing perhaps that no one of good faith would
believe the charges. Instead, he is focused on a more important tribunal, which he will face shortly upon entrance into eternity.

Alberto is palpably grateful for the time he has been given to
"get right with God." He beseeches his family to see the situation as
God sees it — as a gift and cause for joy — and promises to intercede
from Heaven. He gently scolds them for their tears, reminding them
that his entry into Heaven is a most joyous occasion.

[23] Courtesy of Brigade 2506 Museum.

✠ ✠ ✠

Virgilio Campaneria Ángel also entered eternity on that fateful day. His testimony reads as a love letter to his country.

La Cabaña, Cuba, April 17, 1961

To my fellow students and to the people of Cuba in general:
At this moment I am waiting for the sentence of the court that judged me. Death does not worry me, because I have faith in God and the destinies of my country. My death will be another step backwards for those who believe that they can drown with blood the yearning for freedom of the Cuban people. I do not fear it, let death come; I am going happy because now I see my homeland free, now I see how my brothers jubilantly climb the glorious Hill, there will be no more hatred between brothers, there will be no more throats asking for a wall. Everything will be love between Cubans, love of brothers, love of Christians. Poor Cuba, how much you have suffered, but the new Cuba arises from hatred to sow love, from injustice to sow justice, social justice, not deceitful demagogy of the people; a mature Cuba because it already knows all the deceptions and fakers; a Cuba for Cubans and "with everyone and for the good of all."

You, student, have the glory of liberating the Homeland and raising that new Cuba. LONG LIVE CHRIST THE KING! LONG LIVE FREE CUBA! LONG LIVE THE REVOLUTIONARY STUDENT DIRECTORATE!

Virgilio Campaneria Ángel[24]

---

[24] "Cartas antes ad Ser Fusilados de Virgilio Campanería, Rogelio González Corzo y Alebarto Tapia: Testigo del Sacrifico, April 28, 2011, Baracutey Cubano, http://baracuteycubano.blogspot.com/2011/04/cartas-antes-de-ser-fusilados-de.html.

Virgilio's letter is more militant than the others, with strong exhortations to the remaining student members of the MRR to continue the fight. His testament has distinct political overtones, cutting to the core of the corrupt communist system. It also serves as a manifesto of the MRR. His confidence in the future shows that the MRR was not simply an anti-communist league: it also presented a real alternative for governing Cuba. Virgilio's beliefs recall the original purpose of the MRR—to recover the revolution—in an increasingly quixotic effort to right the course.

Its ranks were full of bright would-be leaders who had plans for Cuba's future, who thought themselves better equipped to handle the challenges that faced the nation, and whose vision for the ends of government—stability, justice, the common good—was rooted in practical measures virtuously attained. Interestingly, Virgilio describes a better future for Cuba that can only be achieved through the consent of the governed, not through communism. In one stroke, he destroys communism's claimed monopoly on utopia by demonstrating Castro's cruel distortion of the revolution's own principles.

Virgilio employs cutting irony to illustrate how communism destroys all of its purported aims. The final few lines dramatically illustrate these disparities: "Everything will be love between Cubans, love of brothers, love of Christians."

Fraternal love is a core principle of communism—at least on paper and in propaganda. The fact that Virgilio writes of brotherly love as he is condemned to an unlawful death by his "brothers" is not lost on the reader. "The love of Christians," a self-sacrificing love, calls to mind his ultimate sacrifice for God and his countrymen—as opposed to the ersatz and disordered love of man espoused by communism.

"Poor Cuba," says Virgilio, "how much you have suffered, but the new Cuba arises from hatred to sow love, from injustice to sow justice, social justice, not deceitful demagogy of the people." Here he strikes a death blow to the core lie of communism, a lie that "Catholics" who support communism often have recourse to: that is, the cry of social justice.

The Catholic Church's teaching on social justice has been deliberately misinterpreted and weaponized by socialist and communist regimes worldwide. Liberation theology is one such distortion. An excessive focus on things of this world—the alleviation of poverty at all costs, even the cost of freedom, at the cost of your soul—leads to the worship of man.

It is one of the many diabolical twists of communism that it sought to appropriate Catholic social teaching to its own ends. Liberation theology took a deep hold in all of Latin America. One of the MRR's strong positions was a commitment to true Catholic social teaching, refusing to fall for the Trojan horse of liberation theology. The MRR's energetic activism and track record of Catholic Action initiatives are further evidence of this integrated understanding of Catholic social teaching.

Virgilio demonstrates in one sentence the discrepancy between true social justice and the communists' "deceitful demagoguery." Manipulation and false promises are the currency of communism. Recognition is the first step of resistance. The freedom fighters' ability to see through quotidian government lies strengthened their resolve to resist the Father of Lies at the final moment.

Virgilio ends on a practical note, leaving the reader to ponder the failures of Castro's regime in light of his outsized promises to promote the common good. It is a rhetorical reminder that "By their fruits you shall know them."

Virgilio expresses confidence that the tide is turning—turning toward "a mature Cuba because it already knows all the deceptions and fakers; a Cuba for Cubans and 'with everyone and for the good of all.'" He believes that the Cuban people have been fooled long enough; they see Castro for the liar and fraud that he is, and they recognize that the common good, so often preached by communists, is more likely to be achieved in a freely governed Cuba.

Finally, he entreats the students of the MRR to revel in the nobility of their cause: "You, student, have the glory of liberating the Homeland and raising that new Cuba. LONG LIVE CHRIST THE KING! LONG LIVE FREE CUBA! LONG LIVE THE REVOLUTIONARY STUDENT DIRECTORATE!"

His vision for a free Cuba has sadly not yet come to fruition.

✠ ✠ ✠

Eight in La Cabaña

In like manner, the remaining prisoners were led to be executed. All but one.

Tomás Fernández-Travieso was one of the eight in "the chapel" (cell) that day, yet his death sentence was commuted to thirty years in prison because he was only seventeen. The communists feared the PR nightmare of executing a minor. Tomas writes that at this moment, he realized his role in the MRR had forever changed. He keenly felt the responsibility he now shouldered to preserve and tell the stories of his martyred comrades. He writes of Rogelio: "I became the repository of his memories, the link with life. I would be the witness of his sacrifice."[25]

Tomás served nineteen years in prison, and was freed as part of a plea deal negotiated by the president of Venezuela. He is a teacher,

[25] Ibid.

a writer, and a playwright. One of his plays, *Prometheus Unchained*, was performed in Miami while he was still in prison, earning him an additional sentence for its perceived dissident message. He has written a novel about the intrigue and drama of the counter-intelligence movement, *Beyond the Silence.*[26]

✠ ✠ ✠

The Cuban community has not forgotten the sacrifice of these men. There was talk of opening a cause for canonization for Rogelio, Alberto, and Virgilio, which so far has not advanced beyond preliminary stages. Miami's Francisco Human Rights Park bears Rogelio's codename.[27]

Assault Brigade 2506

The culmination of all of the efforts of the Cuban resistance was the Bay of Pigs Invasion, conducted April 17–20, 1961.

The Cuban freedom fighters, trained by the CIA offshore for months, were organized in Assault Brigade 2506. With 1,414 members, the brigade was a force to be reckoned with. All members were young Cuban exiles ready to liberate their homeland.

It was named in memory of Brigadier #2506, Carlos Rodriguez Santana, after his death during training. The numbering system actually started at 2501, to give the enemy the impression that their numbers were much larger than they were.

The brigade was composed of these former *agruppados* and MMR members, professionals, and former Cuban military personnel who had become disillusioned with the Castro regime. The brigadiers

---

[26] Ibid. See Tomás Fernández-Travieso, *Beyond the Silence* (Scotts Valley, CA: Createspace, 2015).

[27] Francisco Human Rights Park, https://www.miamidade.gov/parks/francisco.asp.

were filled with a realistic optimism: they were well-equipped, well-trained, and had been promised American help.

In addition to their military aims, many devout Catholic brigadiers spent the months of training preparing spiritually as well. The brigade was equipped with four priests, administering to the spiritual needs of the men and ensuring that the cause remained noble and that the members always saw beyond political aims to recall the Four Last Things.[28]

During training in Guatemala, the priests offered Mass continuously for the freedom fighters. Inspired by Cuba's national patroness, La Virgen de Caridad del Cobre, the brigadiers set up a shrine to her, modeled on the national shrine back home.

Ricardo Sanchez, veteran of the invasion, remembers one such priest: Fr. Tomás Macho Castillo, S.J., who served as a chaplain as well as paratrooper. "Fr. Macho" had been a teacher at Belen Jesuit. He was a devoted shepherd of souls and a Cuban patriot. He had been involved with Catholic Action at the school; now was the time to practice what he preached.

Ricardo amusedly remembers one scene: Due to his priestly duties, Father did not have time to train with the brigade on military matters as frequently, and was somewhat ill-equipped the day of the invasion. In a parachute jump, his parachute cord wrapped around his arm, severing his bicep in two. He survived— and so did his arm—but the muscle was completely split, so that when he flexed, it appeared "like a camel." This earned him much ribbing—and respect—from his flock of freedom fighters.

Brigade member Frank de Varona's 2013 obituary for Fr. Macho recalls a harrowing experience during the invasion itself.

[28] Triay, *Bay of Pigs,* 14.

Fr. Macho carried a portable Mass kit in a small black suitcase, and he said Mass in the direst of circumstances. During the Bay of Pigs Invasion, when his small group had been wading through the Cuban swamps without food or water for four days, Fr. Macho opened his suitcase to offer a special Mass, marked in the missal for times of great danger. A boat of enemy soldiers arrived at the same time, but their compatriots came to their rescue: brigadistas ambushed the boat, protecting the little Mass.[29]

✠ ✠ ✠

The Bay of Pigs Invasion has gone down in history as a political misstep, setting the scene for the Cuban Missile Crisis several months later.

President John F. Kennedy blundered the mission, inexplicably changing the site of invasion to the almost inaccessible bay at the last minute, refusing air support, and always seeking to maintain plausible deniability. After building trust with CIA contacts for so long, the brigade felt abandoned and betrayed. They were sent into a battle they could not win, and lied to along the way. It is a slight that still reverberates throughout the Cuban-American community.

As the invasion fell apart, about 115 members were killed in action, and the remaining brigadiers would be captured and imprisoned at the infamous La Cabaña. Their fate was at first uncertain: they were all tried and sentenced to thirty years each, but they also represented a useful Cold War bargaining chip. The brigadiers were ultimately released after just twenty-one months in prison, in a deal negotiated by President Kennedy. Kennedy offered $53 million in food and supplies to the people of Cuba in exchange for

---

[29] Frank de Varona, "Padre Tomás Macho Castillo, SJ," August 16, 2013, Gaspar, El Lugareño, http://www.ellugareno.com/2013/08/padre-tomas-macho-castillo-sj-por-frank.html.

the brigade's release. They made their triumphant return to Miami in December of 1962.

✠ ✠ ✠

The prison experience of the brigade members mirrored that of the general political prisoners, albeit in a shorter term.

Rafael Montalvo, president of the Brigade Museum, notes that those twenty-one months in prison afforded an opportunity for increased prayer and meditation. "There was nothing else to do!" he laughs. Many of those who went into prison lukewarm in their faith emerged strengthened and convicted. As did many in the political prisons on the island of Cuba, the prisoners of the brigade dutifully recited the prayers of the Mass, even when the consecration was impossible. Montalvo also recalls that families would sometimes smuggle in consecrated hosts during visiting hours so the prisoners could receive Our Lord in the Eucharist.

Triay writes, "The aura of the Roman Catholic Church and its open opposition to Communism clearly emboldened even those anti-Castro fighters and Brigade members who may have only been nominally Catholic before the revolution."[30]

In addition to prayer, the brigade's mission sustained them. They kept their hymn close to their hearts:

Nothing will hold back
this War of Ours
for it is a holy war
and we go with the Cross
Let us break the chains
The Fatherland awaits us[31]

[30] Triay, *Bay of Pigs*, 15.
[31] Ibid., 185.

The prison staff, as always, denigrated any displays of faith. One spiteful guard taunted Fr. Macho, attempting to induce apostasy using the tactics noted earlier. "Do you believe in God? Deny him!" he demanded. Fr. Macho bravely refused, looking down and gritting his teeth. Just as the crowd provoked Our Lord as He hung on the Cross, sneering that He should beg Elijah to help Him, the guard cackled, "May Saint Peter come down with his keys and get you out!"[32]

Relics from the Prison

A number of religious artifacts survived the brigade's twenty-one months in prison.

Among the artifacts are a half dozen rosaries made by the prisoners out of whatever supplies were at hand—including, fittingly, a cigar box!

The relics of the prison system also include a brown scapular, missals, religious art produced in the camps, and copies of the Bible and the breviary.

When the members of the brigade were released, they were granted amnesty and repatriated to the United States, most settling in the Cuban expat enclave of Miami. To this day, their fight continues. The veterans operate the Bay of Pigs Museum in Little Havana, where they guide guests through the events of that day, the actions of the brigade, and their experience under communism more generally.

They maintain a positive, cheerful attitude, and an unwavering dedication to their ongoing cause. The site is a living history museum, with the history-makers themselves there to interpret and give insight into their own incredible stories.

---

[32] Ibid., 154.

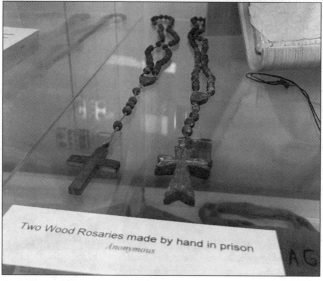

Two Wood Rosaries made by hand in prison
Anonymous

Scapularies used in prison to remind the wearer of commitment to Christian life

In Montalvo's speech on the anniversary of the Bay of Pigs in April 2023, he emphasized that the brigade's work did not end with the invasion. With a museum expansion scheduled for the next several years, they continuously work at their original cause to win support for a free Cuba.

"The Brigade is fulfilling our promise," he said. "Jamás abandonaremos a nuestra Patria." (We will never abandon our homeland.)[33]

Veteran Ricardo Sanchez remembers the combination of meekness and strength that characterized Catholic resistance. In true imitation of Our Lord, the brigadiers were wise as serpents, gentle

---

[33] Rafael Montalvo, "Letter from the President, Rafael Montalvo" (2023), Bay of Pigs Brigade 2506 Museum, https://www.bayofpigsbrigade2506.com/letter-from-president-rafael-montalvo.

as doves. Ricardo notes that "the photos of the dead at the museum are the most important things we have. *We* were able to live our lives."

The author with brigade veterans

*Assault Brigade 2506's flag, carried into battle at the invasion and later presented to President Kennedy
Photos by the author, courtesy of the Bay of Pigs Museum*

Shrine to Nuestra Señora De La Caridad

Every Cuban-American has a story to tell about communism. Many experienced it directly; all have family who did. Many have family who still do. Cuban-Americans are able to send assistance to their Cuban family members stuck on the island, where corruption, poverty, and censorship still keep the people in chains.

Miami is a Cuban city. The expat community is strong, vibrant, and positive, despite the continued oppression of their homeland. They are also deeply Catholic, conscious of the great privilege of living in a place where the right to freedom of worship is protected. One of the central spiritual sites of the Cuban community in Miami is the Shrine of Our Lady of Charity (*Nuestra Senora de la Caridad*), otherwise known as Our Lady of Cuba or La Virgen del Cobre.

Built in the 1960s, the shrine is located at the edge of the property of St. Kieran's Catholic Church, flanked by a Catholic hospital, school, and former monastery and convent.

As with many Marian titles, the origin of Our Lady of Caridad de Cobre can be traced to a miraculous appearance of Our Lady. Rather than a heavenly visit, this title began with a miraculous *image* of Our Lady that materialized out of the ocean.

As the story goes, three seventeenth-century fishermen from El Cobre, each known as Juan (*los tres Juanes*), embarked for the Bay of Nipe in northern Cuba to get salt for preserving meat. They were set upon by a storm, far from land. The youngest Juan, still a child, was wearing a medal of Our Lady, and urged his companions to implore her protection. The storm suddenly abated, and the three Juans noticed a bright object floating on the horizon. As it came closer, they saw that it was a statue of Our Lady holding the Child Jesus, with an inscription, "Yo soy la Vírgen de la Caridad." She is venerated on September 8, the feast of Our Lady's Nativity.

The three Juans brought the statue to El Cobre, where a chapel was erected. Public veneration began soon after, with many miracles attributed to her intercession. In 1936, Pope Pius XI permitted a canonical coronation for the statue, providing further official status. The shrine in El Cobre became a national, and then an international site of pilgrimage.

In a fascinating twist, the Castro regime never touched the shrine during his persecution of the Church, expulsion of priests, and seizure of religious sites and property. Perhaps due to nostalgia, PR concerns, or a deep knowledge that the site was beyond his power, Castro opted to preserve the shrine, even visiting on several occasions. The shrine has also been a primary location of papal visits to Cuba.

✠ ✠ ✠

Wherever the Cuban people go, there goes the Virgen del Cobre.

The members of Brigade 2506 set up a duplicate Shrine to Our Lady of Charity at their training camp in the Florida Keys.

The image of Our Lady's rescue of the three Juans, afloat in the ocean, runs deep in modern Cuban history. The image of the stranded boatmen cannot help but call to mind the freedom fighters and refugees desperately making the ninety-mile journey from Havana to Florida. Driven by complete faith and a radical trust in God, they complete their harrowing journey.

A statue of Our Lady would make this harrowing journey herself. In 1961, a group of Cuban exiles arranged to smuggle a statue of Our Lady of Charity from the Guanabo parish in Havana to the United States. Smuggled through a diplomatic suitcase via the Panamanian embassy, Our Lady arrived triumphantly in Miami on her feast day, September 8. Work began on the shrine in 1966, and devotion has steadily grown. Pope John Paul II even visited the site in 1987.[34]

---

[34] "History," National Shrine of Our Lady of Charity, https://www.ermita.org/CatholicChurch.php?pg=Sanctuary_History&lg=SP.

The statue smuggled from Cuba behind the altar at the shrine. The mural behind the altar was painted by Teok Carrasco. It includes scenes from Cuban and Church history. One panel depicts an angel carrying the Cuban flag to Heaven.

Bishop Roman

The shrine will forever bear the marks of Bishop Agustín Román, a giant of the Cuban diaspora and pillar of the Miami community, who developed the shrine and shepherded the diocese until his death in 2012. His former secretary remembers Bishop Román as a warm man, an enthusiastic catechist, and a skillful evangelist. He died one morning in the shrine's parking lot, just before a full workday, serving his apostolic mission to the end.

Bishop Román was born in Cuba in 1928. He was ordained in 1959, just before the revolution took hold. When Castro came to power, then-Fr. Román was outspoken against the regime. He was persecuted and imprisoned for a short time before being expelled from the country. Undeterred, he served as a missionary in Chile for

several years, and eventually came to Miami in 1966.[35] The exiles, many of whom had suffered under Castro's anti-Catholic measures, were overjoyed to have such a strong witness for the Faith at the helm of the Cuban community.

✠ ✠ ✠

Perhaps one of the greatest contributions of the Church in exile was Operation Pedro Pan, a Church-sponsored refugee program for Cuban children that provided a life of opportunity in the United States. Between 1960 and 1962, over fourteen thousand children

[35] "Most Reverend Agustin Roman," History, National Shrine of Our Lady of Charity, https://www.ermita.org/CatholicChurch.php?pg=Msgr+Agustin+Roman&lg=SP.

fled communist Cuba unaccompanied, some as young as six years old. They were resettled in Miami and hundreds of other American cities, some with family members who had already been exiled, others in foster care.[36]

✠ ✠ ✠

Nestled in neighborhoods between parks and shops, sunflower vendors dot the streets of Little Havana. They make their way home through the sunny streets to the shrine of Our Lady of Charity. Pilgrims and community members make their daily offerings to Our Lady, producing a joyous living garden.

Archdiocese of Miami blogger Antonio Fernandez muses about the significance of the sunflower as a Marian symbol: just as the sunflower turns its face toward the sun, Mary always looks toward Our Lord, from whom she gains her purpose and her life.[37] The sun as the symbol of the Resurrection enhances the analogy, as we recall Jesus' Easter victory over death and Our Lady's crushing the head of the serpent.

This theme of victory over evil has translated into the sunflower's new political meaning for Cubans. In what has come to be known as the "Sunflower Revolution," Cuban citizens have protested peacefully on the feast day of Our Lady of Charity, September 8, since 2018, to "reject the Castro-communist tyranny and its policies that have created profound misery, injustices and oppression"[38] and call for the release of

[36] Victor Triay, *Fleeing Castro: Operation Pedro Pan and the Cuban Children's Program* (Gainesville: University Press of Florida, 1999).

[37] Antonio Fernandez, "Sunflowers and Our Lady of Charity," Let's Talk, September 2, 2019, https://www.miamiarch.org/CatholicDiocese.php?op=Blog_15672153739765.

[38] "CubaBrief: Cachita, the Sunflower Revolution, and Her Legacy of Freedom in Cuba," Center for a Free Cuba, September 9, 2020, https://www.cubacenter.org/archives/2020/9/9/cubabrief-cachita-the-sunflower-revolution-and-her-legacy-of-freedom-in-cuba.

political prisoners. Protestors combine religious procession with cultural festival and human rights activism, indelibly marking the sunflower as a symbol of prayers for freedom. In this light, the deep devotion of Cuban-American pilgrims to the Miami shrine takes on a new significance as each flower represents not only a pious act of public veneration but also a national plea for the liberation of their countrymen.

Every experience of communism—even within one country—is different in degree but the same in kind. There are as many different experiences of communism as there are survivors of communism. Each sunflower offered to Our Lady of Charity, each weapon smuggled, each day of starvation in the prison, each Mass in circular six, each protest derives its temporal effectiveness from its spiritual foundation: *¡Dios, Patria, y Vida!*

The motto of the Cuban diaspora emblazoned at the shrine.

Resources

Cuba is one of the few remaining communist regimes. The behavior and policies of the Cuban government consistently raise flags on Human Rights Watch. According to an article originally published by the *Latin American Tribune*, of the island's 6.7 million baptized Catholics, only 2 percent are considered practicing (attending weekly Sunday Mass): an absolutely devastating decline.[39]

To learn more about the ongoing repressions, how a communist state operates in the twenty-first century, and how you can help, visit the websites of the following organizations:

Center for a Free Cuba

A coalition of scholars, human rights activists, and policy advisors, this non-profit seeks "to promote a peaceful transition to a Cuba that respects human rights and political and economic freedoms."[40]

The Center publishes a regular Cuba Brief, a repository of Cuban history and cultural resources, dissident art and writing, and a directory of pro-democracy Cuban voices today. It also sponsors

[39] Ibid.
[40] "Who We Are," Center for a Free Cuba, https://www.cubacenter.org/who-we-are.

petitions, including the bold "Expel Cuba from the UN Human Rights Council" of April 2022.

Brigade 2506/Bay of Pigs Museum

This is the museum that I visited and where I met with many veterans. As the veterans age, the museum is making efforts to record all their stories and expand educational resources. A new building is being planned.

Other Museums and Cultural Centers

Casa del Preso

This small house museum highlights the plight of Cuban political prisoners from 1959 to the present day, with special advocacy for the release of current prisoners.

Museum of the Cuban Diaspora

Celebrating the accomplishments of the Cuban diaspora across the globe, with monthly exhibits on notable Cubans in all industries.

Victims of Communism Memorial Museum

The recently opened museum features a reconstructed Cuban prison cell as part of its interpretation of oppression in Cuba.

CHAPTER THREE

Czechoslovakia

*"Even though they didn't say anything, the features on their faces
when they came back from prison stayed in my memory forever."*

— František Mikloško on the return of political prisoners

*"In the 1950s and 1960s, we lived more on
intuition than on verified information."*

— Mikloško on the secret Church

CLOSED IN BETWEEN two genocidal totalitarian empires in what
historian Timothy Snyder has christened the "Bloodlands," Czechoslovakia bore particular witness to the tumultuous twentieth century.
The Church has strong roots in Czechoslovakia, which once
belonged to the Habsburg Empire. Sts. Cyril and Methodius — "the
Apostles to the Slavs" — performed most of their mission work in
the Czech and Slovak lands. The Church suffered in this country
after the Hussite revolt in the fifteenth century, but it remained
active. Today, the Slovak nation is known for its loyalty to the
Catholic Church.

The Slovak National Uprising of 1945, in which the Slovak
people sought to overthrow their Nazi-collaborating government,
was portentous of the decades of resistance to come. Many dissident

clergy were imprisoned by both the Nazis and the communists for their refusal to collaborate with evil in any form.

After the Allied partitions of World War II ceded Czechoslovakia to Soviet control, a 1948 coup cemented the country's communist fate. Following a Stalinist model, atheism became the official state ideology overnight, thus relegating centuries of Catholic life to the funeral pyre of progress.

František Mikloško's experience under communism was one of heroic, public resistance. Born in 1947, just a year before the communist takeover of his homeland, he never knew a Czechoslovakia without communism — that is, until he helped to create it. From the 1970s, he was involved in anti-communist action, culminating in the Velvet Revolution of 1988. He spearheaded the 1988 Candle Demonstration in Bratislava, a catalyst for the Velvet Revolution, the first domino to fall behind the Iron Curtain, ultimately hastening the collapse of the U.S.S.R. Mikloško and his colleagues worked directly with Pope John Paul II to support Vatican-loyal priests and reinvigorate the faith of the besieged Czechoslovak populace. Unwavering loyalty to the Catholic Magisterium guided their daily choices. Careful diplomacy, intellectual formation, and faith in action characterize Mikloško's resistance to communism.

Fittingly, he continued his work of diplomacy in the newly democratic and independent Slovakia, serving as the first Speaker of the Slovak National Council. He founded and led the Slovak political party Conservative Democrats of Slovakia, which arose from the Christian Democratic Movement, and he ran for president three times — in 2004, 2009, and 2019. He is now retired from politics and is writing his own accounts of the Catholic Church and Catholic resistance in communist Czechoslovakia, which will be available for Czech and Slovak readers in the coming months.

František was born on June 2, 1947, in Nitra, a mid-sized Slovak city about sixty miles east of what is now Slovakia's capital city, Bratislava. He was born just one year before the communist takeover of Czechoslovakia in those politically chaotic postwar years. His father held a doctorate of law, but he taught in secondary schools all his life. His mother was a professor of Slovak and French. She also taught in secondary schools, but then stayed home to raise her four children, of which František was the youngest.

The Mikloško family in the late 1950s. František kneels in front.

Mikloško describes his mother as a deeply religious person, active in literary and translation projects despite recurring illness that caused her death at the age of fifty-four. She took a particular interest in church activities, helping to produce a small magazine for the local parish and playing as an organist at Mass.

František fondly remembers his postwar childhood. In Czechoslovakia, as everywhere in Europe, the standard of living was modest after the war. But despite the challenges, he recalls his childhood as joyful and carefree. The family was happy to perch just outside the hustle and bustle of the city, enjoying the pleasures of simple country life.

The family lived on the outskirts of the city, on a hill called Kalvária (Calvary), where there was a pilgrimage church to the Mother of God, Our Lady of the Assumption. It is a common pious tradition in Slovak towns to adorn the local hill with a church and name it Calvary—a sign of the people's deep Catholic roots. Nitra itself is the oldest bishopric in Central Europe, and was the location of the first Christian church in Slovakia. To many, it is considered the mother of Slovak cities.

Until 1950, the Nitra Kalvária was also home to a monastery of the Society of the Word of God, otherwise known as the Verbists. Due to its robust Catholic history, Nitra was also home to several high-ranking Church dignitaries.

Notably, the Kalvária was a Marian pilgrimage site, hosting a special annual pilgrimage to the Mother of God every August 15. Pilgrims attended from far and wide, but it was especially popular among the people of neighboring villages, of both Slovak and Hungarian descent.

František recalls the impression these festive pilgrimages made on him as a young boy: "This, along with the stalls selling various religious items and the 'beggars' who were an integral part of every pilgrimage, created an unrepeatable color of events and experiences for a small boy like me."

As we will see, the Nitra pilgrimage would play a role in the collapse of communism many years later.

František notes that the most important aspect of his Catholic upbringing was his mother's religious education. He and his siblings

The Nitra Kalvária in the 1950s

attended public school, as parochial schools were not common in the area. So the majority of religious education was undertaken at home and through involvement at the church.

František speaks of the fun they had, led by their mother, marking the liturgical year: "Together with her, we experienced the entire church year like children and with joy: Advent, Christmas, Lent, Easter, the feasts of the Mother of God and the like." He credits his mother's strong faith with his lifelong adherence to Catholicism. Even as a teen and young adult, he did not experience any doubts or rebellions against the Faith, even in a country where to do so had become a badge of national honor.

It is clear that Nitra was truly a Catholic city, with a religious pedigree second to none and a thriving community of clergy, religious, and laity. František spent countless hours of his childhood in this pious enclave.

But trouble was brewing. Ever since the communists had taken power, the Catholic stronghold at Nitra was operating on borrowed time.

Kalvária, Calvary

Operation K

This idyllic Catholic atmosphere was soon to be interrupted. The year 1950 marked one of the most brutal anti-Catholic operations undertaken by the Czechoslovak government. In a sweeping move, the government shut down over 90 percent of the country's monasteries, seizing 219 monasteries and deporting and imprisoning 2,376 monks. Operation K derived its codename from *kláštery*, the Czech word for *monasteries*. It was an anti-Catholic, specifically anti-clerical pogrom.

As in Cuba, a primary move taken by communist governments is to isolate and attack the clergy. The clergy are the lifeblood of the Church: their apostolic succession ensures they are acting *in persona Christi* in providing sacraments, leading, and administering to the faithful. No clergy, no Mass, no Real Presence, no absolution, no sacraments of any kind, no visible Church. In a sick way, anti-Catholic governments of all kinds understand this theology. By targeting the clergy first, they cut off the laity not only from their shepherds, structure, and leadership, but also from the very things integral to the daily practice of their faith. The Faith lives on in extraordinary circumstances, even when the faithful are deprived of the sacraments, but governments certainly try to smother it.

Operation K took place primarily on two nights, April 13–14 and May 3–4.

Over the course of years, they were herded into work camps, conscripted as forced labor in factories, and imprisoned, marking a religiously targeted human rights abuse on the scope of the early Nazi years.

The same brutal course of action was deployed against convents later in 1950, taking the name "Operation R," from the word for *nuns, řeholnice.*

Operation R was arguably more ruthless than Operation K, at least in magnitude. Over four thousand nuns were forcibly removed from their orders and pressed into labor at factories. While nuns were considered less of a threat to the government than monks (and certainly less than priests), they were not spared the same full persecution and attempted suppression of their vocation. In addition to arrest, deportation, and practical enslavement, the nuns, as women, suffered indignities repugnant to their state in life: Sr. Teodora, a survivor of Operation R, revealed to Radio Prague International in a 2020 interview that men would routinely undress between the machines where the sisters were working, with no regard for modesty.[41]

The contemplative orders bore the brunt of the persecution, as they were considered useless to a work-obsessed proletariat dictatorship. Religious who served a state-sanctioned "function" as teachers, nurses, or public servants of some kind were occasionally allowed to keep their work.

This reduction of the religious, once a very respected institution in Slovakia, to their utilitarian value as laborers betrays the completely materialist view that characterizes communism. This is the dark side of utopia: production at all costs, a stripping of the human person to his Stakhanovite value. Atheist utopia has no regard for the next life; prayer is useless. Heaven is already here, or in the making. And it is created through work. The state expected to replace God as master of these monks' and nuns' lives. Their devotion and selflessness were manipulated for crooked ends.

One can imagine the great merit affixed to the sacrifice of the religious who suffered under this unfair yoke.

---

[41] Brian Kenety, "Operation Ř: How the Communists Targeted Czechoslovakia's Nunneries," Radio Prague International, July 29, 2020, https://english.radio.cz/operation-r-how-communists-targeted-czechoslovakias-nunneries-8687793.

These policies are reminiscent of Habsburg emperor Joseph II's "reform" of the monasteries in the eighteenth century, in which he severely restricted the activities of the contemplatives because they did not "contribute" to society. Joseph II, unfortunately rejecting his traditional Catholic upbringing, was steeped in Enlightenment ideals that would find their future fulfillment in communism.

✠ ✠ ✠

Anti-clericalism (like anti-Catholicism in general) runs deep in all communist regimes, regardless of geography. But Slovakia has a uniquely interesting recent past that may have colored how the clergy were perceived in the wake of World War II.

I asked Mikloško about Czechoslovakia's particularly virulent vein of anti-clericalism, wondering about its origins. Hypothesizing that Slovakia's fraught history of clerical fascism might have contributed, I inquired about the role of Josef Tiso, Slovakia's wartime priest-dictator, in the development of the overall image of the clergy.

Tiso was a Slovak priest who became president in 1939. He was eventually tried and executed for treason by the Czechoslovak government in 1945. His crimes were numerous. He was a Hitler sympathizer, and, unhappily, committed his nation to a Nazi alliance that decimated the country's Jewish population and soured relations with the Vatican. Pope Pius XII's view of Tiso was evident in a message sent through his delegate at the time: "The injustice wrought by his government is harmful to the prestige of his country and enemies will exploit it to discredit clergy and the Church the world over."[42]

---

[42] Quoted in Livia Rothkirchen, "The Churches and the Deportation and Persecution of Jews in Slovakia" (2000), Shoah Resource Center, Yad Vashem, https://www.yadvashem.org/odot_pdf/Microsoft%20Word%20-%20697.pdf

The pope's prediction proved prescient. Tiso was certainly a convenient propaganda tool for the communists. The narrative that "priest equals fascist" could be easily put forward, and severe actions could be taken in the name of "denazification."

Denazification, while initially a legitimate Soviet goal, soon became the catchall excuse for many human rights abuses under Eastern European communism, capitalizing on the traumatized citizens' suffering during the war. The Soviets did play a role in bringing actual Nazi war criminals to justice: In addition to participating in the Allied-led Nuremberg Trials, the Soviet government independently conducted its own tribunal against Nazi collaborators. In the Krasnodar Trial of 1943, during the war, eleven Soviet men were convicted of collaborating with the Nazi *Einsatzgruppen,* the Eastern Front's SS branch, which was responsible for the mass murder of thousands of Jews by gun and traveling gas van, independent of the camps.

The specter of remaining Nazi fifth-column elements in newly won Soviet lands led to paranoia among Soviet leaders. They began to see Nazi sympathizers behind every rock. Moreover, they found a convenient way to demonize anyone who disagreed with them as "enemies of the state."

Often employed against individuals who had nothing to do with Nazism, or weren't even alive during the war, the charge soon lost its meaning as a precise accusation. Interestingly, this feeble and duplicitous charge is still being used by the Russian government today: "denazification" was one of the official reasons the Putin regime gave for the 2022 invasion of Ukraine. For anyone familiar with the long history of this terminology, *denazification* is synonymous with "fake communist accusation."

Given the cry-wolf attitude that communist governments took toward liberally applying the term *Nazi,* it would appear that Tiso's actions were not a significant deterrent to the practice of the Catholic Faith in Slovakia. Mikloško does not believe Tiso turned the populace against the priests. Respect for priests ran too deep to be thwarted by one man. Additionally, to counter Tiso's example, there were countless Slovak priests who heroically resisted both Nazi and communist atrocities.

One such example is Josef Beran, the eventual archbishop of Prague who, as a bishop in 1945, denounced the Nazi regime from the top of St. Vitus Cathedral. For his resistance, he was deported to the priests' block in the concentration camp at Dachau. Surviving the camp, he returned to his post, only to be imprisoned again, this time by the communists. In 1951, Beran was put through a show trial for his crimes against the state, which included a refusal to swear allegiance to the communist government (an act that, to Beran, constituted treason to the Catholic Faith). He also prohibited priests under his jurisdiction from swearing this allegiance, condemning the Czechoslovak nationalist church (the wing of the church that went along with the communist agenda) as a schismatic fraud. He refused to resign, despite immense pressure from collaborating clergy and laity. He was freed in 1963, but was kept under a close watch by the communists. Elevated to the cardinalate by Pope Paul VI in 1965, he went to live in Rome, alleviating some of the pressure from the communist state. He took part in the final session of the Second Vatican Council and died of lung cancer in 1969.

✠ ✠ ✠

Despite the persecution of strongly Catholic Nitra, the Mikloško family still kept the Faith. Pilgrimages and traditions continued, even when the monastery was suppressed.

The suppression of the monastery hit close to home. František vividly remembers a night in 1950, when his family was paid a visit by the secret police. Due to his mother's involvement at the parish, the police seemed to believe that she must have some secret knowledge about clandestine Church activities, or that the monks had hidden some Church property or money in the house. The atheist militants proceeded to question the family and ransack the house. It was a traumatic experience for the young boy. He can still see the man in the long black trench coat and hear his father's whispers to his mother, too afraid to speak aloud. Three-year-old František, not knowing any better, handed a small prayer book to one of the police. This supremely ironic act became a running joke in his family for years to come.

This was hardly the last encounter with the secret police. Mikloško writes, "My whole childhood was connected with the fact that someone was always arrested in our neighborhood." The family constantly coped with the anxiety of the unprovoked raids, arrests, and intimidation.

František calls to mind the feeling of dread that arose when the distinctive Tatraplan cars of the secret police (the Czechoslovak version of the Soviet police car known as the "Black Maria") were spotted in the neighborhood. On one such occasion, a neighbor casually commented, "They are taking another victim." The situation had become routine and played out as if from a script. The unlucky victim would be taken away—sometimes for a few hours (and a few beatings), other times for years, returning to his devastated family when he no longer recognized them.

Mrs. Mikloškova was friends with many priests from Kalvária and the surrounding countryside, several of whom were arrested as dissidents. The family visited one such priest upon his return from the prison. Even in the small, dim room, the priest was on edge and afraid, too fearful to speak aloud. František struggled to hear the priest as he whispered his account to his mother. What was this evil force that could reduce grown men—his intelligent, accomplished father, and a strong, holy shepherd of Christ—to pitiful whispers?

František marks these incidents as formative moments in his assessment of communism: "Because of this experience from my childhood, I never believed in communism. I carried the conviction that communism persecutes God and His faithful and is therefore evil from the beginning."

✠ ✠ ✠

The Czechoslovak National Church: Anti-Catholic Propaganda

The first thing the communists tried to do after the February 1948 coup was to create the so-called "national church," separated from the Vatican and subservient, both doctrinally and institutionally, to the Czechoslovak Socialist Republic. It is estimated that a total of 11.5 percent of clergy collaborated with the regime in this way.[43]

Readers will recognize this tactic from our study of Cuba, where this plan took the form of liberation theology. In Czechoslovakia, this shadow "anti-Church" was even more delineated in its structure and hierarchy.

From the beginning, this scheme was accompanied by an intense campaign of anti-Catholic propaganda. The Communist Party developed the slogan "Turn away from Rome, toward a national church."[44] Whereas members of the new "national" church — mercenaries who served the regime — were celebrated and promoted for

---

[43] Felix Corley, "The Secret Clergy in Communist Czechoslovakia," p 191. He cites a newspaper as follows: *Lidove noviny* (Prague), quoted in *The Warsaw Voice*, 31 May 1992.

[44] Scott Vitkovic, "The Clandestine Catholic Church (Ecclesia Silentii) in Czechoslovakia during Communism (1948–1991)," paper presented at Howzeh Elmiyeh Conference, Qom, Iran, March 2022, https://www. researchgate.net/publication/359142598_THE_CLANDESTINE_ CATHOLIC_CHURCH_ECCLESIA_SILENTII_IN_CZECHO-SLOVAKIA_DURING_COMMUNISM_1948_-1991.

their compromised doctrine, faithful Catholics were scorned and derided for clinging to their "retrograde" faith. Newly unacceptable beliefs included allegiance to the pope, contemplative prayer, popular piety, and anything that could be considered a "bourgeois superstition," especially devotion to the Real Presence.

One particularly formative propaganda victory occurred in the aftermath of the miracle at Číhošť and the subsequent show trial of 1949.

The town of Číhošť is a tiny Bohemian village of three hundred inhabitants, about sixty miles southeast of Prague. Its small but pious Catholic population witnessed a miracle during the homily at Mass on December 11, 1949. The priest, Fr. Josef Toufar, was preaching passionately about the Real Presence. At a certain point he pointed to the tabernacle and uttered these words: "Here in the tabernacle is our Savior. There the merciful Heart of Jesus lives, beats and awaits us sinners." At that moment, the cross hanging above the tabernacle began to sway back and forth, and remained bent forward after it stopped moving. Father, facing the people to deliver the homily, did not see this happen. He was soon informed by the approximately twenty parishioners who witnessed the miracle, and by the next day the village was abuzz with the news. Fr. Toufar continued with his duties in preparation for Christmas. As he was offering the Christmas Mass, the miracle occurred *again*. At this point, Fr. Toufar knew he had to report this extraordinary occurrence to the local bishop for investigation and potential authentication. But the Church authorities weren't the only ones listening. The secret police (StB) soon caught wind of the miracle, and in early January knocked on the rectory door, under the guise of requesting a tour of the church. As they turned the corner behind the cemetery walls, they arrested Fr. Toufar and took him to prison in Valdice.

Over the next month, he was interrogated, beaten, and tortured within an inch of his life. Fr. Toufar was subjected to brutal torments such as beatings, electric shocks, sleep and food deprivation, and being forced to walk for miles when he could barely stand. The StB wanted him to sign a statement confessing that he had faked the miracle at Číhošť. He refused. Even if the miracle turned out to be nothing more than a natural event or an optical illusion—it had not yet been properly investigated by the Church—it was certainly not a deliberate counterfeit, and he would not lie. He could not in good conscience confess to a crime he hadn't committed. Even if it saved his life, he knew the scandal that such a lie would cause to the Church, shaking the faith of untold numbers of Catholics. This is where Fr. Toufar's true heroic virtue lies: not in his witness of a miracle, but in the refusal to bear false witness. In the refusal to compromise the foundational doctrine of belief in the Real Presence. And in the refusal to become a propaganda pawn of the atheist regime.

Just as John the Baptist died protecting virtue and marriage and Thomas More died defending the papacy, Fr. Toufar died defending one principle of the Faith, but died *for* Truth—the whole Truth of the Catholic Faith.

Through it all, he could be heard singing hymns in his cell.[45]

✠ ✠ ✠

This incident inspired the propaganda film *Alas for the One through Whom the Umbrage Comes*, which tried to discredit the miracle (and, along with it, the entire Catholic Faith), by claiming that Fr. Toufar had faked the miracle at the behest of his Vatican handlers.[46]

[45] Sr. Zdenka Mᵃ Turkova, S.H.M., "Fr. Josef Toufar (1902–1950)," *HM Magazine* 173 (September–October 2013), http://bosilkov.com/en/museim/otets-yozef-toufar-1902-1950-144.

[46] Thomas McEnchroe, "'Operation K': How the Communists Wiped Out Czechoslovakia's Monasteries in One Brutal Stroke," Radio Prague International, April 13, 2020, https://english.radio.cz/operation-k-how-com-munists-wiped-out-czechoslovakias-monasteries-one-brutal-8103215.

And the StB's plot for Fr. Toufar's involvement went even further than soliciting a false confession. The plan was to force Fr. Toufar to re-enact on film how he had "invented" the miracle. This would involve an elaborate rope and pulley system showing how the cross was purportedly moved, not by God but by a trick of man. Fr. Toufar was too unwell to be forced into the project, so a double was used.[47] This hit piece was used to stir up the populace ahead of a trial that brought Fr. Toufar before a state tribunal. In a farcical show trial, he was accused of anti-state activities, of fomenting loyalty to the Vatican over loyalty to Czechoslovakia. This paranoid trial evinces another aspect of communist hatred of the Church: as an *institution* competing for fealty. In addition to the supernatural chasm between an officially atheist state and a "backwards" religion, the political angle of anti-Catholic action was a convenient pretext for suppression of Church activities. In a totalitarian system, the state is the supreme good; any other loyalties pose an existential threat to its very existence. Any Catholic swearing obedience to the pope was considered to be a member of a dangerous and revolutionary fifth column.

The ultimate purpose of the trial was to justify Operation K, initiated just three months later, and concomitant anti-Catholic operations. Along with the suppression of the monasteries, the government swiftly moved to expel all foreign priests, and paved the way for arbitrary arrest of clergy for a new crime, the "promotion of superstition."

The propaganda narrative was simple: Catholic priests had, for centuries, deceived the proletariat with their superstition and false promises. The Church is counterrevolutionary and must be eliminated. When you're yearning for Heaven, and taught to offer up sufferings, you won't agitate for change in this life. Furthermore,

[47]   Turkova, "Fr. Josef Toufar."

the dogma of the primacy of Peter—to which all Catholics are bound—means that all Catholics, but especially clergy, are nefarious foreign agents with competing loyalties. Ideologically, this all makes sense. But now, there was "proof"—on film, no less.

It is difficult to judge how successful the film's clunky ideological narrative was in turning the populace against Catholics. More often, any surge of support for the communist system grew out of fear, helplessness, or opportunism, rather than sincere ideological conviction. The film was a smokescreen, to check a box that no one was expecting, to create a flimsy excuse for an action no one could stop anyway, to lend paltry legal justification to the unjustifiable.

On February 25, 1950, Fr. Toufar's health began to decline rapidly. The StB transferred him to a clinic in Prague, where doctors unsuccessfully attempted to save his life. He succumbed to his injuries, utterly deformed by the tortures. The official cause of death was peritonitis.

As the *National Catholic Register* reported, Fr. Josef Toufar's cause for beatification was opened in 2015.[48] What are believed to be his remains were exhumed from a mass grave outside Prague for examination as part of the Church's official investigation. Czech historian and priest Fr. Tomáš Petráček serves as postulator for the cause, and has written extensively about Fr. Toufar, his witness as a martyr, and his place in the historiography of Czechoslovakia under communism.[49]

Czech historian Miloš Doležal full biography of Fr. Toufar, *As If We Die Today*, is available to Czech and Slovak readers.

---

[48] Bohumil Petrik, "Czech Priest Witnessed the 'Cihost Miracle' and Was Killed for It," *National Catholic Register*, February 25, 2015, https://www.ncregister. com/news/czech-priest-witnessed-the-cihost-miracle-and-was-killed-for-it.

[49] Tomáš Petráček, "The First and Second Life of Father Josef Toufar (1902–1950) and Shifts in Interpretations of Modern Czech History: On One Unexpected Phenomenon in Contemporary Czech Society," *Kirchliche Zeitgeschichte* 29, no. 2 (2016): 355–369, https://www.jstor.org/stable/44254205.

The Returnees

This is the besieged atmosphere in which the priests of Czechoslovakia were operating from 1949 onwards.

As Mikloško describes it, priests—and laymen—returning to Nitra from prison generally did not want to talk about their experiences. When they left prison, they usually had to sign a statement promising their silence, to maintain the image of a free and democratic society. In addition to this, they experienced so much human humiliation in prison that they didn't want to go back to it.

"So, we only imagined the details," Mikloško says. Sometimes, the family was afforded glimpses into the horrors of the prisons. There was an StB facility in Nitra, and František remembers once hearing a desperate cry from the depths of the building. There was an unspoken acknowledgment whenever a neighbor was hauled off to prison, and a general feeling of unease upon their return. As Mikloško remembers, "Even though they didn't say anything, the features on their faces when they came back from prison stayed in my memory forever."

For Mrs. Miškoškova, the risk was even greater. Prompted by her conscience, she began to get involved in samizdat publication of dissident materials. From the Russian words *sam* (self) and *izdat'* (to publish), the word refers to the clandestine self-publication of dissident materials behind the Iron Curtain. Its counterpart, *tamizdat*, refers to material published abroad (*tam* meaning "there") and smuggled back into communist countries.

Mrs. Miškoškova was always aware that she could be arrested at any moment. František remembers that she had a parcel of basic linen and hygiene supplies ready, just in case.

In 1960, his mother was proofreading a samizdat religious text, a recent translation from French. News of this project somehow reached the secret police, who searched the Miloško residence again. Miraculously, she was not arrested, and they left without additional incident. The regime could be as capricious as it was cruel.

Miloško speculates that his mother may have received a certain degree of protection due to her respected status in the local community. She was known for her great social awareness and generosity of spirit. For years, she had been the godmother to several Roma children—a risky move under the Nazi regime—and made sure they were well-fed whenever they visited.

Similarly, his father was spared persecution in the realm of employment. As a respected instructor of science, he held the position of director at a secondary medical school. He managed to hold on to this position even once his public opposition to communism became well known.

At the beginning of the 1950s, Mr. Miloško was hauled before the State Security and pressured until late at night to sign cooperation with the party. He boldly refused.

Despite this, he kept his position at the medical school, and his children could attend school. Why did the authorities leave him alone? Again, František must rely on speculation. Mr. Miloško was a soccer referee for a local team and played cards with the leaders of the school in Nitra. But these connections don't seem elevated enough to pull strings. He never compromised. He publicly attended Mass and lived out the Faith.

The Miloškos' relatively easy experience in keeping employment and higher education was unusual for practicing Catholics, who were usually denied entrance to such institutions on account of their Faith and lack of party membership. In the next chapter, we will discover the story of a Czech woman who struggled to maintain enrollment or employment for precisely these reasons.

So, Mikloško remains perplexed at the fact that his family was spared this particular trial. It was certainly not due to any form or degree of collaboration or backhanded deals, however. After the fall of communism, citizens had the opportunity to review their state security files. František decided to view his father's file, and was pleased to learn that the State Security had always had his father marked as a "person hostile to communism."

✠ ✠ ✠

The Czechoslovak National Church: Catholic Action Subverted

As mentioned before, in communist Czechoslovakia only obedient state priests could be elevated to higher positions within the Church. Through this tactic, the bishoprics were gradually seeded with collaborators hostile to the true Faith.

The 10 percent of clergy loyal to the regime congregated in the euphemistically named "Peace Committee of the Catholic Clergy in Czechoslovakia." This organization would undergo several re-brandings, including the "Pacem in Terris" of the 1970s–1980s, but remained in force until the collapse of communism. As we shall see, the group was explicitly excommunicated for their treason to Rome and the Faith by Pius XII in his 1949 decree. Subsequent versions of the group also incurred excommunication ipso facto, the last decree being issued by John Paul II in 1982.

Never popular among the people, the group operated by the force of the communist state alone. Good Catholics often knew to avoid these collaborator priests, as they had avoided the "juring priests" of the French Revolution's Reign of Terror. It is estimated that up to twenty-five thousand Czechoslovak citizens participated in uprisings throughout 1949 to protest the national church measures.[50]

✠ ✠ ✠

The communist propagandists employed a wily narrative to justify these hostile and anti-Catholic actions. They attempted to co-opt the idea of Catholic Action, launched by Pope Pius XI in the 1920s as an answer to Pius X's call "to restore all things in Christ." As we saw in Cuba, true Catholic Action consisted of social movements that sought to bring Christ into the public sphere, evangelize the world, and restore the social kingship of Christ. The communists, in subverting and appropriating Catholic Action to their own nefarious purposes, attempted to maintain a veneer of Catholicity under which to preach their anti-Catholic doctrines. They perverted the principles of Catholic Action, replacing them with a man-made, man-centric gospel of materialist prosperity and ersatz fraternity.

This lie was rather a stretch. In fact, Pius XI's 1931 encyclical *Non Abbiamo Bisogno* (We do not need…) was actually written to encourage Catholic Action *against* rising communist factions in Italy.[51]

The Popes against Communism

The Vatican issued several decrees around the middle of the twentieth century that made the Church's position on communism clear and provided support to Catholics trapped in communist regimes.

[50] Lukáš Obšitník, "Veriacism zakazal citat statne Katolicke novitny. Odsudili ho za velzradu" (He forbade the faithful to read the state Catholic newspaper. He was convicted of treason), Konzervatívny Denník Postoj, September 2, 2016, https://www.postoj.sk/16771/veriacim-zakazal-citat-statne-katolicke-noviny-odsudili-ho-za-velezradu.

[51] Pope Pius XI, Encyclical Letter on Catholic Action in Italy *Non Abbiamo Bisogno* (June 29, 1931), https://www.vatican.va/content/pius-xi/en/encyclicals/documents/hf_p-xi_enc_29061931_non-abbiamo-bisogno.html.

For our purposes, the most important among these are:

1. The promulgation of *Divini Redemptoris* by Pius XI

2. The excommunication of communists by Pius XII

3. The "Secret Mandates" of Pius XII

The first of these documents was Pope Pius XI's 1937 encyclical *Divini Redemptoris*, a treatise "On Atheistic Communism" addressed to the bishops of the world. Pius XI writes "with particular affection" for the people of Russia, Spain, and Mexico, who had recently survived communist upheavals in their respective countries:

> Where Communism has been able to assert its power—and here We are thinking with special affection of the people of Russia and Mexico—it has striven by every possible means, as its champions openly boast, to destroy Christian civilization and the Christian religion by banishing every remembrance of them from the hearts of men, especially of the young. Bishops and priests were exiled, condemned to forced labor, shot and done to death in inhuman fashion; laymen suspected of defending their religion were vexed, persecuted, dragged off to trial and thrown into prison.[52]

The fate of Catholics in these countries, as described here, was played out in all other countries that fell to communism as if from a playbook.

✠ ✠ ✠

Divini Redemptoris condemns communism in no uncertain terms. Pius XI points out that no sooner had the term *communism* been

---

[52] Pope Pius XI, *Divini Redemptoris*, no. 19.

invented than it had been condemned by previous popes, including Pius IX, Leo XIII, and Pius X:

> The Communism of today, more emphatically than similar movements in the past, conceals in itself a false messianic idea. A pseudo-ideal of justice, of equality and fraternity in labor impregnates all its doctrine and activity with a deceptive mysticism, which communicates a zealous and contagious enthusiasm to the multitudes entrapped by delusive promises.[53]

He continues: "Communism, moreover, strips man of his liberty, robs human personality of all its dignity, and removes all the moral restraints that check the eruptions of blind impulse."[54]

Here the Holy Father shows he is aware of the infiltration of Catholic institutions, precursors to the national churches:

> In the beginning Communism showed itself for what it was in all its perversity; but very soon it realized that it was thus alienating the people. It has therefore changed its tactics, and strives to entice the multitudes by trickery of various forms, hiding its real designs behind ideas that in themselves are good and attractive.... They try perfidiously to worm their way even into professedly Catholic and religious organizations.[55]

The encyclical concludes with an exhortation: "See to it, Venerable Brethren, that the Faithful do not allow themselves to be deceived! Communism is intrinsically wrong, and no one who would save Christian civilization may collaborate with it in any undertaking whatsoever."[56]

---

[53] Ibid., no. 8.
[54] Ibid., no. 10.
[55] Ibid., no. 57.
[56] Ibid., no. 58.

✠ ✠ ✠

As communism's diabolical aims became more obvious and the threat more existential, Pius XII, Pius XI's successor, raised the stakes. On July 13, 1949, the Vatican published a decree excommunicating ipso facto anyone who professed or adhered to communist doctrine. The rather vague language of the decree brought into question who, exactly, would be considered a communist by these standards. Yet Pius XI had made it clear in *Divini Redemptoris* that ordinary people who happened to fall under the yoke of a communist occupation were not to blame for their geographic misfortune:

> In making these observations it is no part of Our intention to condemn *en masse* the peoples of the Soviet Union. For them We cherish the warmest paternal affection. We are well aware that not a few of them groan beneath the yoke imposed on them by men who in very large part are strangers to the real interests of the country. We recognize that many others were deceived by fallacious hopes. We blame only the system, with its authors and abettors who considered Russia the best-prepared field for experimenting with a plan elaborated decades ago, and who from there continue to spread it from one end of the world to the other.[57]

But now, through the lies, schemes, and double-talk of communists, and the desperation of confused citizens, the line was becoming blurred between Marxist true believer, collaborator, ordinary citizen, and persecuted faithful.

These judgments were typically left to the bishops, who already made prudential judgments about worthy reception of the Eucharist in caring for their flocks. Pius XII's strong language did cause some

---

[57] Ibid., no. 24.

confusion as to who exactly was excommunicated, especially in the complex psychological torture chamber of choices between compliance and resistance. Many decisions were made under extreme duress that most people can only imagine. Only God can judge hearts.

It seems that excommunication was primarily reserved for those Catholics who officially cooperated with communist governments in matters of personal advancement—especially clerics, whose responsibility to uphold the Faith was greater. Therefore, in the wake of the decree, there were several cases in which it had to be clarified or firmly enforced.

One of the first of these was in Czechoslovakia: the case of Fr. Ján Dechet. Fr. Dechet accepted a promotion from the communist government to the position of "administrator" of the Banska Bystrica region. The term *administrator* was an obfuscation: the reason the region needed to fill such a role was that its bishop had just died. Essentially, the Czechoslovak government was installing its own bishops, a schismatic act. Pius XII saw right through this and excommunicated Fr. Dechet, offering a revocation if he resigned his position. It is unclear what Fr. Dechet decided to do. He never officially renounced his position or publicly disavowed communism, but he did leave Banska Bystrica. He died, with the matter unresolved, in Bratislava in 1968.[58]

In Czechoslovakia, the excommunication was applied liberally to the members of the so-called "Catholic Action," or "Peace Committee." On the whole, Mikloško considers the communists'

---

[58] Jozef Haľko and J. Pešek, "Chapter Vicar Jan Dechet: A Symbol of the Violence of the Communist Regime in Czechoslovakia Directed Towards Subversion of the Catholic Church," *Historický Časopis* 54, no. 2: 287–304, https://www.researchgate.net/publication/294385064_Chapter_Vicar_Jan_Dechet_-_A_symbol_of_the_violence_of_the_communist_regime_in_Czechoslovakia_directed_towards_subversion_of_the_Catholic_Church.

presumptuous usurpation of Catholic Action to have been a hubristic failure. He counts Pius XII's decree of excommunication as a great victory in protecting the true Faith.

There still was a shadow-church of collaborators, and they still wielded real power, but at least now Catholics knew, without any doubt, where they should stand if they wanted to save their souls. While its status would later become more complicated, the Czechoslovak national church was, for now, officially schismatic.

Following this propaganda campaign, the communists' next strategy was to strike at the heart of the Church by attacking the bishops—in the spirit of "Strike the shepherd, and the sheep will be scattered" (Zech. 13:7).

Mikloško addresses the immense pressure that the government placed on bishops, even those who initially remained loyal to the Vatican. The communists played the long game, gradually inducing a slow apostasy:

"It should be added that the bishops who remained 'free' gradually changed their tactics and, from an uncompromising attitude towards the communists, slowly became loyal. Thus, two lines of church life were born in Czechoslovakia and Slovakia, the line of martyrs and heroic followers and the line of bishops and priests who lived at different levels with the regime. Both lines lasted until the fall of communism."

After the mass arrests of the monks, priests, and now bishops, it is estimated that 50 percent of Czechoslovak churches were left without clergy. The clergy that remained free were under constant psychological pressure to collaborate. With the clergy so threatened, the Church's very existence was at risk. A remedy was to come in the form of the clandestine Church.

Secret Mandates

Pius XII's strongest act of support for the persecuted churches came in the form of the "Secret Mandates" of 1948–1950. The mandates provided blanket jurisdiction for all Catholic bishops living under the yoke of communism to consecrate bishops, ordain priests, and perform their ministries without explicit permission from the Holy See.[59] The mandates were a great help to clandestine churches throughout communist territories, from the Soviet Union to Vietnam.

Another decree came from Pius XII directly to the bishops of Czechoslovakia. It was addressed to Bishop Štěpán Trochta, bishop of a suburb of Prague, who had been active in the resistance against Nazi occupation and survived internment at several Nazi concentration camps. Beyond a simple toleration, Bishop Trochta was *mandated* to consecrate additional bishops, one for each diocese, to ensure apostolic succession in the event that the primary bishop was arrested and killed.

Bishop Trochta was himself eventually confined to house arrest in 1950, arrested in 1953, and began serving a twenty-five-year sentence in 1954. During this time, he was able to consecrate a handful of secret bishops. He was tortured and killed during a police interrogation in 1974.

The Underground Church: Ecclesia Silentii

Formed by his early impressions of the evil nature of communism, František Mikloško was naturally attracted to the secret Church.

---

[59] Scott Vitkovic, "The Czech Republic: From the Center of Christendom to the Most Atheist Nation of the 21st Century, Part 1, The Persecuted Church: The Clandestine Catholic Church (Ecclesia Silentii) in Czechoslovakia During Communism 1948–1991," *Occasional Papers on Religion in Eastern Europe* 43, no. 1 (January 2023): 19–59, Geroge Fox University, Manuscript 2400, https://philarchive.org/archive/VITTCR-2.

As a student, he began to approach the clandestine clergy for the sacraments, and gradually became involved in the activities of the secret Church.

Mikloško describes the origins of the secret Church:

> In Slovakia, Roman Catholic bishops Ján Vojtaššák and Michal Buzalka and Greek Catholic bishop Pavol Gojdič were arrested and sentenced to many years in prison. The other bishops became so isolated in their residences that they completely lost contact with their priests and believers. In these dramatic moments arose the so-called secret church. From the ranks of the Slovak Jesuits, priests were secretly ordained as bishops, first Pavol Hnilica, who was ordained a bishop in the hospital by Bishop Róbert Pobožný of Rožnav, who was there as if on a medical examination. Then Hnilica secretly ordained Ján Korec, whose story is known around the world and who became a Nitrian cardinal after the fall of communism.

From left to right: Mikloško, Cardinal Tomášek, Bp. Korec, and Ján Čarnogurský

Ján Chryzostom Korec in his apartment with the anti-eavesdropping apparatus he used to outwit surveillance while speaking with friends. He knew his apartment was almost certainly bugged. Ca. 1980s.

Other bishops secretly consecrated at this time included František Tomášek, who also became a cardinal after the fall of communism. Mikloško and his associate Silvestr Krčméry worked very closely with Bishop Korec. Another leading figure in the movement, Ján Čarnogurský, would get involved in post-communist politics, becoming prime minister in 1991.

Ján Chryzostom Korec was a young Jesuit priest from Bošany, a town near Mikloskoʾs native Nitra, secretly ordained in 1950. Only a year later, Korec was secretly consecrated a bishop in 1951 at the age of twenty-seven. At the time of his consecration, he was the youngest Roman Catholic bishop in the world. He was in prison from 1960 to 1968. He ordained more than a hundred secret priests in his lifetime, several of them in prison. Korec wrote extensively during these years, publishing samizdat religious texts and disseminating them among the Czechoslovak faithful. In his life, he wrote over sixty volumes, including a memoir of his persecution called *The Night of the Barbarians*. He was released from prison during the Prague Spring and eventually made a cardinal by John Paul II in 1991.

The cadre of secret bishops continued the vital work of the Church under constant threat of arrest and death. They provided the sacraments, instructed the faithful, ordained priests, and even organized a seminary in case the extreme situation persisted. The lay members of the resistance were also responsible for writing, transcribing, and disseminating samizdat literature, facilitating the secret study of religion, and organizing peaceful demonstrations.

Safeguards were put in place to protect the identities of the members, especially the priests. Nevertheless, the simple daily tasks of Catholic sacramental life became deadly risks. The Church operated in the catacombs for the protection of its own members.

One particular challenge was the constant presence of the StB agents, who were aware of the clandestine church and attempted to infiltrate these secret circles. The use of informants was a tool of coercion and control employed across all communist states. Ordinary citizens were pressured and incentivized to spy on their neighbors, friends, and family. Many were power hungry, motivated by petty jealousies or fantasies of revenge. Others were motivated by fear. After communism fell, Eastern Bloc countries made citizens' surveillance files available for viewing. Learning who had informed on you was a shocking and isolating experience.

The informant culture sowed division and distrust within communities, neighborhoods, even families. It fostered a culture of paranoia; you never knew who you could trust. The underground Church was not immune to this. In fact, the StB had specifically targeted the secret Church as a surveillance subject and is known to have sent multiple agents, posing as devout Catholics, as spies. Mikloško discusses the ubiquity of these spies:

> The phenomenon of agents of the State Security did not become public until November 1989. Until then, we only suspected that some people were causing caution by their behavior. The secret bishop Korec told me that in the Jesuit order, where he belonged, he became very friendly with one gifted, clever brother. They went for walks together and debated philosophical questions. After the abolition of religious orders in 1950, this young person was imprisoned for a while. When he returned, he looked for young Ján Korec and in the conversation Korec found out that he had been sent by State Security to find out some information. That person then made a great career in life, but Korec never met him again. In the 1950s and 1960s, we lived more on intuition than on verified information.

Rather than being crippled by this situation, saturated in distrust, the secret Church forged ahead.

When asked why he chose to remain in Czechoslovakia rather than attempt to flee, Mikloško responds:

> I never thought about escaping from Czechoslovakia. In my entire personal, religious, and later political life, the most important thing for me was friendship with the people I worked with. I found inner freedom even in totalitarian life. I also got to know excellent literature and great art in totality. I often felt threatened, but basically I was always happy. Some of my friends, the secret priests, went to the West to help us from there. I took it as a sacrifice on their part, not as leaving for a better and more comfortable life.

His attitude evinces the close fraternity and shared mission of the underground Church.

Years later, Mikloško assesses the critical role the secret Church played in preserving the Faith: "If there was no secret church and the faithful were only under the influence of collaborating priests, after the fall of communism the church in Czechoslovakia would probably be in the same state as the Orthodox church in Russia is today—i.e., spiritually disorganized."

It is truly a grace that the true Catholic Church in Czechoslovakia remained largely free from communist error, even if reduced in number and grandeur. As Mikloško indicates, the Russian Orthodox Church was a different story, and was almost completely infiltrated by KGB agents. Kirill, the current patriarch of Moscow and a close ally of Putin, is a former KGB agent (as, of course, is Putin himself). Ironically, the relegation of the true Church to the catacombs provided a layer of doctrinal protection: while attempts at infiltration of the underground Church were made, the false national church served as a repository for all anti-Catholic elements. The doctrinally compromised stayed with the national church. Those willing to risk their lives for the integral Catholic Faith, whole and inviolate, approached the secret Church. But even among these august ranks, the devil was at work.

The Underground Church: Breakaway Elements

Czechoslovak Catholics faced almost insurmountable struggles in locating the sacraments. Not only did they have to avoid the national priests, but they had to be wary and discerning in approaching men who claimed to be clandestine clergy as well.

After Pius XII's mandates, secret consecrations abounded. Due to the secretive nature of the consecrations, the identities, episcopal lineage, and supporting documentation of the secret clergy were often obscured, if available at all. This secretive, chaotic atmosphere presented unique challenges in vetting candidates, ensuring doctrinal orthodoxy and personal virtue, and keeping track of sacramental lineages.

Ordinations occurred discreetly, often in plainclothes, in hotel rooms, parks, or private residences. As a security measure, witnesses were rarely present. Historian Felix Corley has written that the candidates for the priesthood or the episcopate would sometimes not even be informed of the identity of their ordaining bishop, as an added layer of protection should one of them be arrested.[60]

The edifying stories of hero bishops such as Korec suggest that all underground priests were virtuous martyrs, unwaveringly orthodox and ready to sacrifice for the Church. But history paints a much more nuanced story.

In reality, the chaos that ensued in the underground Church exemplifies the Scripture "Strike the shepherd, and the sheep will be scattered" (Zech. 13:7).

---

[60] Felix Corley, "The Secret Clergy in Communist Czechoslovakia," *Religion, State and Society* 21, no. 2 (1993): 171–206.

In the absence of direct lines of communication with the Vatican, and under the constant pressure of state surveillance, the underground Church was, by its very nature, not a monolithic, organized force. Within the circles that comprised the clandestine Church, several competing factions arose, of varying degrees of reliability and certainty in sacramental validity.

"Every Man a Pope"

The underground Church was essentially divided into two camps. One remained loyal to the Vatican and understood that the Church was only operating "underground" out of extreme duress. This is the group Mikloško was involved in, under the tacit leadership of Bishop Korec. The Korec group exercised discretion in all their actions, especially in deciding the future of secret ordinations. They understood that these were emergency measures, only intended to last the duration of the crisis of communism. They sought communication with the Vatican and eventually worked with Pope John Paul II in the 1980s.

The second group consisted of the followers of Felix Maria Davídek, whose increasingly non-Catholic actions caused the Korec group to distance themselves from them.

Davídek was ordained a priest in 1945, several years before the coup. He was secretly consecrated a bishop in 1967 by clandestine bishop Jan Blaha. For years, he contributed to the perpetuation of the Church under persecution.

But then he went rogue. Seemingly motivated by a desperation for clergy, Davídek began to use unconventional methods to continue apostolic succession. First, he began ordaining married men to the priesthood. His methodology and use of a loophole in this effort seemed dishonest, as though he was trying to trick God. Davidek would cunningly use the Eastern Rite of Ordination, as the Eastern Slovak Greek Catholic Church allows married priests. Purportedly, the men would be sent east to minister to the Eastern Catholics in Slovakia, but this often did not happen. The newly ordained priests would instead go on to function essentially as priests of the Latin Church (in which the ordination of married men is forbidden), celebrating Mass according to the Roman Rite.

Davídek used the emergency as an excuse to undertake increasingly unorthodox measures. This approach culminated in Davídek's "ordination" of several women to the priesthood. For years, even after the fall of communism, this information was suppressed. In the melting pot of misinformation, it was difficult to discern whether this intelligence was true, or a communist invention to discredit the Church. In 2001, Davídek's secretary Ludmila Javorová published a memoir that dispelled these doubts. Ludmila admitted to having been "ordained" by Davídek, ostensibly to be able to minister to women in gender-segregated concentration camps. The Vatican has since declared her ordination to be certainly invalid, upholding Catholic teaching on the priesthood.

Davídek is reported to have formed his own personal cult. He cut off ties with underground Church members who did not agree with his maverick approach and doctrinally liberal views. Even before these allegations came to light, the Vatican ordered Davídek to cease and desist episcopal duties in 1978.[61]

Davídek's prideful and presumptuous actions may have been motivated by a sincere desire to save souls, but in his blind zeal he violated Catholic principles. His anti-communism overrode his adherence to the Catholic Faith. He essentially created his *own* faith, his own church, in which priesthood took on a novel definition. Davídek assumed powers far beyond his state in life. Hence

---

[61] Burton Bollag, "Clandestine Priests in Czechoslovakia Lose Vatican Status," *International Herald Tribune*, April 13, 1992.

the historian Franz Gansrigler's assessment of the Davídek wing, which was encapsulated in its title: *Every Man a Pope.*

Through extensive interviews and investigative research, Gansrigler traced the many episcopal descendants of Davídek, many of whom were working regular jobs and no longer exercising their priestly function. In turn, they were spurned by the Vatican. Gansrigler concludes that there are more questions than answers when it comes to the status of these supposed priests. The insistence of some of Davídek's followers on forging their own path independent of the Vatican essentially devolved the duties of the papacy to the individual, reminiscent of Protestant errors about the supremacy of individual conscience over the primacy of Peter.[62]

Davídek's story demonstrates that all resistance to tyranny must be first and foremost grounded in a strong foundation of objective belief. It is not enough to stand against injustice; one must stand *for* truth.

What's more, evidence has emerged that the StB was constantly trying to infiltrate secret Church circles. Some Catholics involved in the hidden Church even claim that the heterodox factions supporting married clergy and women's ordination were communist infiltrators seeking to discredit the underground Church.

The convoluted story of the factional underground Church shows the dangers endemic to operating outside of ordinary jurisdiction. Corley, quoting Fr. Dubovsky, a secret priest, observes that "a church founded on secret bishops would make sense only if one believed that 'in ten years everything would be over.'"[63] But as the communist tide rolled on, and the number of bishops proliferated, the web became even more tangled.

---

[62] Franz Gansrigler, *Jeder War Ein Papst: Geheimkirchen in Osteuropa* (Salzburg: Otto Müller, 1991).

[63] Corley, "Secret Clergy."

✠ ✠ ✠

This chaos caused many laymen to doubt the validity of their sacraments. This confusion continued into the twenty-first century, as the Church in the former Czechoslovakia reorganized itself. From the collapse of communism in 1989, efforts to regularize the secretly ordained clergy have been ongoing. It was determined that approximately 250 priests had been secretly ordained from 1949 to 1989.[64] In the year 2000, Pope John Paul II required the majority of these priests to undergo conditional ordinations.

And so, underground Catholics faced two enemies: the one without, and the one within. The enemy without—the atheist regime—was an obvious foe, almost a caricature of evil. The lines became blurred when dealing with the national church, where psychological warfare tactics made choices less black and white. Catholics caught in-between had to reckon with outward persecution as well as their own weaknesses, often having to fight against their inherently trusting nature when dealing with official clergy.

The government maintained control over the country's two main seminaries. The regime held the powers of apostolic succession captive in this way. Some young men, loyal to the Vatican and the true Faith, nevertheless went through seminary just so they could be ordained and practice as priests. Others considered this too much of a compromise, seeking out the clandestine Church instead.

The Vatican's policy of *Ostpolitik* in the post-Vatican II years, which sought reconciliation and normalization with communism, blurred the national church's formerly clearly excommunicated state under Pius XII.

64 Jonathan Luxmoore, "Re-ordination an Option for Secret Czech Priests," *National Catholic Reporter,* February 25, 2000, https://natcath. org/NCR_Online/archives2/2000a/022500/022500f.htm.

Around the same time, the reforms of the Prague Spring were loosening tensions on the underground Church, expanding the offering of state licenses for priests, and even officially recognizing members of the underground Church.

✠ ✠ ✠

The final frontier against the enemy within was the fight against desperation and its fatal consequences.

Imagine Satan's reaction to a heroic band of clergy and laity risking their lives for the true Faith. Until they are safe in the arms of Our Lord, they are fair game. Satan designed temptations tailor-made to these zealous believers. They had already proven they were not tempted by worldly gain: they didn't care if they lost money, status, or even their lives. And they were not easily confused: they had already proven they could see right through the lies of the national church facade.

So how, then, can they be tempted? Through desperation. Desperation for clergy spurred Davídek's heterodoxy, which culminated in his shocking and invalid ordination of women.

By contrast, the faith of the underground Church under Korec is apparent in its absolute refusal to violate *any* Catholic principles, even when doing so would seem to be necessary to "save" the Church. Bishop Korec emphasized that the underground Church sought only to preserve the Faith until it could be restored to normal operations. John Paul II confirmed the unity of the underground elements who remained faithful to the Vatican with the universal Church.

Korec himself emphasized this unity of faith and ecclesiology in 1987: "There is only one Church. There is likewise only one priesthood."[65] Therefore, the distinction between "underground Church" and official Church was merely a temporal one. When

---

[65]   Corley, "Secret Clergy," 193, n. 109.

understood in this way, the term *Ecclesia Silentii* is truly the most accurate: the underground Church was simply the Church—with no novelty or departure. It was no more and no less than the Catholic Church in Czechoslovakia. It just happened to be silenced.

The fidelity of the orthodox branch of the *Ecclesia Silentii* was rewarded even in this life, as its members orchestrated the collapse of the entire system that condemned men to impossible choices.

The Prague Spring: Czechoslovakia's Laetare Sunday

Peaceful demonstration was a key component of Mikloško's work with the secret Church.

By 1968, such public actions were more and more accessible. This is in large part due to the change in regime. In January 1968, Alexander Dubček was elected first secretary of the Communist Party of Czechoslovakia (i.e., head of state). Dubček's regime adopted the slogan "Socialism with a human face," which sought to modernize and relax the iron grip of the communist system.

He was the author of the Prague Spring, a series of reforms that loosened crippling restrictions on media, travel, freedom of speech, and religious activity. The period immediately following the Prague Spring came to be known as "normalization." For many citizens, it was their first taste of a normal life.

For the Church, the Prague Spring brought hundreds of priests back from the gulags. The clandestine Church was emboldened to operate more publicly. While the progress promised by the reforms was short-lived, anticipating the Soviet invasion of late August, the mood had changed. The genie could not be put back in the bottle.

During the period of normalization following the Prague Spring, Bishop Korec was rehabilitated and released from prison. It is at this time that Mikloško really got to know him. They shared a heritage as Nitra natives, where Korec would eventually be stationed again by John Paul II. He lived near the bishop and aided in the operations of the clandestine Church. Bishop Korec was Mikloško's confessor.

Mikloško writes of this period of great hope:

> The Prague Spring, although it lasted a very short time, had historical significance for the life of Catholics in Czechoslovakia. The Greek Catholic Church, which was forcibly liquidated in 1950, was restored. All the political prisoners were released, and in those few months of joy and freedom, the church and believers regenerated themselves so much that we were able to live from this joy for the next twenty years. In 1988, a Catholic priest and historian in Slovakia, Štefan Šmálik, wrote a small book called "The Great 40-Year Lent of the Church in Slovakia" in *samizdat*. In it, he calls the year 1968 "Laetare Sunday," on which is worn the pink liturgical color in the middle of Lent before Easter and is a sign of joy and hope. That's how it really was.

Dubček's actions did not make him popular with the Soviet Union, which feared the thaw would weaken its influence in the Eastern Bloc. In response to the Prague Spring, Soviet tanks rolled into Czechoslovakia on August 20, 1968.

František was at college in Bratislava, preparing to take a difficult exam in theoretical physics. Ironically, he remembers the day somewhat fondly. When he arrived at the university, the professor was leaving. Then he came back, looked at the exam, said, "Today is a special day," and marked the exam as passed. Mikloško laughingly remembers that, at the time, he couldn't complain much about the Soviet invasion. "The entry of the troops meant a literal shock for many people." He describes what the invasion meant at large:

I know of cases of people from Slovakia who spent time in the Russian gulags between 1945 and 1953, who hid in the following weeks because they were afraid that the Russians would take them to the gulags again. The borders were opened, and tens of thousands of people left as emigrants. At that time, the Western world provided unprecedented help to these emigrants.

Refusing to be discouraged, the underground Church forged ahead even in these new circumstances. One of Mikloško's close associates was Vladimír Jukl, who had been sentenced to twenty-five years in prison for religious activity in 1952 and spent thirteen and a half years in prison. Of his trial, Jukl has stated, "They considered me one of the most dangerous Catholics in Slovakia and sentenced me for high treason and espionage for the Vatican."

Reminiscent of the propaganda trial of Fr. Josef Toufar, the communists continued to levy "Vatican spy" charges against leading Catholics.

Jukl was amnestied in 1965. Another mathematician-turned-dissident, Jukl had become the *de facto* "general" of the secret Church. He was secretly ordained by Bishop Korec in 1971. In contrast to the unconventional methods undertaken by other wings of the resistance, the Korec group remained staunchly committed to the celibate priesthood. Still, discernment was often hurried, out of circumstantial necessity. While the secret bishops could not submit their candidates for the priesthood to the rigorous vetting process used in ordinary circumstances, they did preserve Catholic norms as far as possible, and they fostered genuine vocations. In the secret Church, the discernment process took on another layer when the candidate considered that a vocation to the priesthood was almost certainly a vocation to martyrdom. Jukl wrote of the first moments of his discernment process:

When I was released I was 40 years old and I had nowhere to live (I lived at my brother's place as an emergency). I had nothing to do. I couldn't get a decent job. And then I was still discriminated [against], I had a low salary, I had no chance to advance in [my] career and I was monitored, either by the police or by spies at work. Then, it was time to decide whether I [would have] a family or not.

I realised that building a family wouldn't be a serious choice for me. I was a discriminated person. I didn't want to involve an innocent woman to take the burden of my persecution. I didn't want it. So I was more and more convinced that my vocation was the one Professor Kolaković advised me.[66]

The involvement of such well-educated, thoughtful academics, along with many students, showed that the labors of the true Catholic Action movements were not in vain.

By the early 1970s, Jukl's decisiveness and grit had earned him the responsibility of determining all new directions and tasks in the secret Church. No stranger to suffering, Jukl received the news of the Soviet invasion with equanimity. Mikloško was inspired by Jukl's encouragement to the student activists. "Let's move on!" he said. "The Church does not choose the time in which it is built. We will work in new conditions!"

The spirit of adaptability meant that the secret Church took on a new presence in the public sphere. Public demonstrations and political involvement became a new way of advocating for the Church and for religious freedom more generally. Students, especially, were attracted to the movement. Even with a lifting of some restrictions,

---

[66] Vladimír Jukl, "Story: Vladimír Jukl," My Story, https://www.mojpribeh.sk/pribeh/vladimir-jukl/?lang=en.

they still had to operate in secret, fostering a conspiratorial camaraderie among the members. Building community became an integral part of their work.

Mikloško attended several secret religious outings, often in the form of hikes and other outdoor activities. Despite the risks, he remembers these as joy-filled events.

It is during this period that the Czechoslovak underground Church really began to resemble other public-facing Catholic Action movements, like the *Aggrupacion* student group in Cuba. The secret Church reclaimed Catholic Action from the communists.

After his 1971 graduation from Comenius University in Bratislava, Mikloško continued his work with the Church. With a degree in mathematics, he was able to get a good job at the Slovak Academy of Sciences, despite his "anti-state activities."

But his dissident work did not go without notice. Over the years, he had several run-ins with the secret police. His colleagues and friends became concerned. Once, his colleague asked if it was worth it to live such a life, with a target on his back. How was it bearable—going to State Security for interrogations, being watched, waiting for them to lock him up one day?

He told her that it was, without a doubt, worth it.

Beyond his religious motivation, Mikloško understood the historic significance of his movement. He recognized that the underground priests were an enormous inspiration to all Czechs and Slovaks, showing them freedom in the face of totalitarianism and giving them a future to hope for: "People who maintained their inner freedom in the time of unfreedom and knew how to support others in this freedom, especially young people, grew into huge personalities."

Mikloško speaks of figures in the movement who inspired him in this way. In addition to Bishop Korec and Vladimír Jukl, he will always remember the courage of Dr. Silvester Krčméry, a layman arrested in 1951. Krčméry was tortured in pre-trial detention, he spent three years in prison because he refused to sign false accusations, and in the end he refused to testify altogether. His final speech at the court became a symbol of Slovaks' resistance to communism. In it, he said, among other things: "You have the power in your hands, but we are right!"

This declaration is evocative of St. Athanasius's injunction "They have the buildings, but we have the Faith!" The communists had usurped power in the state and institutional Church — but the Silent Church had kept the Faith. Truth mattered more than any outward glory.

The leadership of the underground Church inspired Mikloško's own involvement in politics. He says, "With these people, I realized how important it is for young people to have their role models, to have someone to lean on along their way."

This breakthrough to the political sphere marked a turning point for the underground Church. This progress would culminate in the collapse of communism. In addition to demonstrations, pilgrimages formed an important part of public anti-communist activity.

1988: Our Lady Comes to the Church's Aid

August 1988 marked the end of the extraordinary Marian year in the universal Church. John Paul II had declared this to be a time for special penances, prayer, and indulgences. The pope wrote:

> By means of this Marian Year the Church is called not only
> to remember everything in her past that testifies to the special
> maternal cooperation of the Mother of God in the work of
> salvation in Christ the lord, but also, on her own part, to
> prepare for the future the paths of this cooperation. For the

end of the second Christian Millennium opens up as a new prospect.[67]

The end of that second Christian Millennium had been a witness not only to great miracles, but also to some of the worst atrocities in human history. Seventy years earlier, Our Lady of Fatima had warned her children of the evils of communism. Now, she was poised to deliver them from these same evils.

Jukl in 1965, after his release from 13.5 years in prison

Mikloško's group organized a final pilgrimage to celebrate Our Lady's year. The destination was to be his childhood parish, the Church of the Assumption, on the Kalvária in Nitra. The Nitra Assumption pilgrimage, which had played such a pivotal role in František's religious formation, dates back at least three hundred years, with a usual attendance of ten to fifteen thousand people. In 1988, more than fifty thousand pilgrims climbed the hill. The atmosphere was electric, portentous of that "new prospect" imagined by the pope.

Cracks were already beginning to form in the Czechoslovak communist system. Despite the Soviet invasion in 1968, Czech and Slovak citizens were pushing back. The tragedy of Jan Palach, a demonstrator who set himself on fire on the streets of Prague during the Soviet invasion, had sparked a series of mass protests and labor

---

[67] Pope John Paul II, Encyclical Letter on the Blessed Virgin Mary in the Life of the Church *Redemptoris Mater* (March 25, 1987), no. 49, https://www.vatican.va/content/john-paul-ii/en/encyclicals/documents/hf_jp-ii_enc_25031987_redemptoris-mater.html.

strikes from which the communist government never quite recovered. News from neighboring Poland trickled in, sharing hopeful stories of the pope's support of the anti-communist Solidarity movement. Everywhere behind the Iron Curtain, passionate Catholics were establishing themselves as a political force to be reckoned with.

Candle Demonstration

There had already been one major political demonstration in the Marian year of 1988, on March 25, the feast of the Annunciation.

In 1987, a Catholic priest was murdered under unknown circumstances in a village in western Slovakia. Foreign Slovaks, especially the famous hockey player Marián Šťastný, decided that on the

Marian holiday on March 25, 1988, they would organize protests against the persecution of the Church in Czechoslovakia in front of Czechoslovak embassies in countries with large Slovak émigré populations.

The secret Church joined in and commissioned Mikloško as organizer in Bratislava. He seized the opportunity to expand the protest, calling for both religious and civil freedom.

The demonstrators expressed three demands: (1) the free appointment of bishops, without state interference; (2) religious freedom in Czechoslovakia; and (3) civil freedom for all in Czechoslovakia. Protestors expressed their agreement with these demands by lighting candles and taking to the streets.

Mikloško directly challenged the communist authorities in a speech broadcast by Voice of America, Radio Free Europe, and Vatican Radio. He explains the significance of the event:

> The demonstration meant something completely new in the life of the secret Church in Slovakia. For the first time, we left religious spaces such as churches and places of pilgrimage and went to the civic square. Moreover, we demanded not only religious but also civil rights for all people. We set a new horizon for our engagement.

The demonstration was to begin at 6:00 p.m. People lit candles, sang the Czechoslovak anthem and the papal anthem, and began to pray the Rosary. "That prayer held that mass of people together," he says.

The police started ramming into the crowd with cars, then brought out the water cannons. The violence quickly escalated. The police chased the demonstrators with dogs and beat them with batons. More than a hundred people were arrested, including several foreign journalists.

Upon hearing of the people's equanimity in the face of this harsh treatment, Mikloško concluded, "After half an hour of demonstration, where violence reigned, the moral winners were those people. They stayed in the square and showed the power of nonviolent resistance, which is probably the strongest weapon that Slovaks have used in their history."

Other corners of the demonstration had a friendlier atmosphere. As is the case in small Slovakia, even during this violence there were "smiling" events. Many young people took part, often in groups that had met at church. It was raining, and the park where they were standing was muddy. Police officers with dogs immediately started chasing them. Dressed nicely for the event, they started running in high-heeled shoes, a comical sight. As one girl was running away from the policeman, the heel of one of her shoes got stuck in the mud. Astonishingly, the policeman and the dog waited until she came back and put on her shoe, then started chasing her again.

Such was the theater of communism.

✠ ✠ ✠

Of course, StB agents had found out about the demonstration before it happened. Mikloško and several associates were detained by State Security during the actual protests and were therefore unable to see the fruits of their labor. As the leader of the Candle Demonstration, Mikloško was kept in prison for two days.

As the demonstration played out, tantalizingly close yet inaccessible through the prison walls, the StB played mind games with him. They would come into the room and scoff, "Your demonstration—it's a fiasco! No one came." They tried again and again to discourage him by downplaying what was happening.

One StB agent had a twinge of conscience. After the end of the demonstration, alone with Mikloško in his cell, he suddenly exclaimed, "The pope will honor you!"

After Mikloško's release, these cryptic words made more sense. On the outside, he learned of the tremendous success of the demonstration. A total of eleven thousand people had attended and protested peacefully, despite police intimidation and violence.

The peaceful protest had proven to ordinary people that they had a voice. There was no going back. The secret Church had found thousands of new allies, and they would coalesce within the next year into an unstoppable force.

To this day, March 25 is honored as Struggle for Human Rights Day in Slovakia.

✠ ✠ ✠

Pilgrims at Kalvária Nitra, 1988. Mikloško (center in the group of three) is joined by Bp. Korec (right)

Given these circumstances, the StB began breathing down Mikloško's neck like never before. Months later, the resounding success of the Nitra Assumption pilgrimage made the StB nervous.

After the pilgrimage, the secret police hauled Mikloško in to State Security and threatened: "Mr. Mikloško, enough! If the secret Church does not stop, we will take action against it!"

These threats were nothing new. The state had been oppressing the Church for almost forty years. With astounding audacity, the communists had killed, maimed, and tortured priests, destroyed religious communities, and terrorized and impoverished laymen. What more could the state possibly do? To a secret Church already purified by years of martyrdom, these threats were meaningless.

Far from being dissuaded, the secret Church took even bolder action.

Velvet Revolution

"In November 1989, we experienced a biblical miracle," says František Mikloško.

Throughout his childhood, his mother had always yearned for what she called a "quiet revolution," that is, a revolution of ideas, won by peaceful demonstration. Such a revolution would not rely on threats and intimidation. These were the tactics of the weak and power-hungry, of communist totalitarians. Rather, the revolution would seek to win hearts and minds. It would involve the entire populace: she often used the slogan "Women, let's go!" to show that defending human rights was a project for everyone. Unlike the communist revolution, imposed on the masses by a small group of violent ideologues, this revolution would start from the grassroots: families, students, and other individuals would advocate for their own freedoms.

This quiet revolution would awaken true patriotism and love of freedom, latent for decades under oppression. Most importantly, it would remind the Czech and Slovak peoples that they had immortal souls. The sleepers would wake. The silenced would find their voice. Thirty-three years after her death, her son fulfilled her wish. The Silent Church would ignite the silent revolution.

The Velvet Revolution, the fall of communism in Czechoslovakia, took place over eleven days, from November 17 to 28, 1989. The name, sometimes translated as the "Gentle Revolution," derives from the nonviolent tactics of the protests.

The revolution followed a pattern of peaceful demonstration that characterized all the anti-communist revolutions of 1989, from the Solidarity Movement in Poland that summer to the fall of the Berlin Wall. The U.S.S.R. itself would dissolve over the next few years.

Mrs. Miloškova's principles found a voice in the slogan of these new revolutionaries: "We don't want violence; *we are not like them*; we want freedom!" In the spirit of the Candle Demonstration, Czechs and Slovaks took to the streets to advocate for their basic rights. The demonstrations culminated in the establishment of the Civic Forum, a political party that united disparate dissident movements.

Within a month, the communist leader Miloš Jakeš resigned, and Václav Havel, a dissident writer, was elected the first president of a free Czechoslovakia.

The swift collapse of the totalitarian chokehold sent shockwaves across the world. Communism had maintained such a complete and total grip on Eastern Europe for half a century. For years, hope was futile and it seemed communism would last forever.

As Mikloško puts it, "In November 1989, we experienced a biblical miracle. This 'eternal' political system collapsed overnight in Europe like a house of cards. I am personally convinced that the chalice of suffering and sacrifices in communist countries has been filled in the eyes of God, and God has thus entered history. This is my deepest life experience; I cannot have a greater one."

The time had come for the Church to come out from the catacombs. The State Security guard's mysterious prediction that "the pope will honor you!" came true. In April 1990, John Paul II visited Czechoslovakia—the first papal visit to Prague. President Václav Havel echoed Mikloško's sentiment as he greeted the pope: "I do not know if I know what a miracle is. Nevertheless, I dare say that right now I am the witness of one."[68]

---

[68] "On This Day, in 1990: John Paul II Became the First Pope to Visit Prague," *Kafkadesk*, April 21, 2021, https://kafkadesk.org/2021/04/21/on-this-day-in-1990-john-paul-ii-became-the-first-pope-to-visit-prague/.

A triumphant papal Mass at St. Wenceslas Cathedral in Prague completed the victory for which the underground Church had fought so long. The congregation included clerics who had been imprisoned just years earlier for saying Mass. John Paul II celebrated another Mass on the Letna Plain just outside of Prague for an audience of five hundred thousand.[69] The plain had been the Communist Party's chosen site for large-scale propaganda demonstrations and theatrics. It was now reclaimed for Christ. The pope's full visit can be viewed on YouTube.[70]

During the visit, Pope John Paul also went to Bratislava. He returned twice over the 1990s. He maintained good relations with former leaders of the secret Church, including Mikloško's close friends Jukl and Krčméry. The pope received Jukl and Krčméry at Castel Gandolfo in 1996.

Reflecting on the lessons and legacy of these years, Mikloško believes that his faith, and the Church, emerged stronger from the persecution:

> This experience fills me with peace and optimism that no political system, no ideology, can threaten Christianity, as long as it is faithful to its mission and is ready to make sacrifices for it. Quick victories are achieved only through struggle and violence; our mission is to be the faithful leaven and salt of the earth and act according to Christian principles wherever life takes us — in politics, the economy, and in ordinary life. Then it will be true, as in the war between the Jews and the Amalekites, that

69 Thomas McEnchroe, "April 21, 1990 — When John Paul II Became the First Pope to Visit Prague," April 20, 2020, Radio Prague International, https://english.radio.cz/april-21-1990-when-john-paul-ii-became-first-pope-visit-prague-8102461.

70 "Papež Jan Pavel II. v Československu 1990," Ondřej Scholtz, April 14, 2019, YouTube video, https://www.youtube.com/watch?v=6Zb6pKw_xwM.

"the Lord is fighting against Amalek from generation to generation" (Exod. 17:16).

Unfinished History

In Slovakia, between 1948 and 1968, more than seventy thousand people were sentenced to more than a collective eighty thousand years in prison for political crimes. The pressure to collaborate and inform tore apart the social fabric of a functioning society. Father turned against son, neighbor against neighbor, communicant against priest. The economic, psychological, and spiritual scars of communism remain to this day. As Mikloško puts it, "We are still just learning to live in freedom."

Spurred by his involvement in the Velvet Revolution, he went on to spearhead several political parties in the infant democracy of Slovakia. From 1989 to 1992, he was a member of the Public Against Violence, a party that emerged from the Velvet Revolution. In the spring of 1992, he joined the Christian Democratic Movement, where together with Ján Čarnogurský he endeavored to define the relationship between the state and all churches in Slovak society. They sought a deep integration between church and civil life, as opposed to the strict separation of church and state observed in the West. During this period, the party achieved many of its goals by working directly with the Vatican and with leaders of other religions.

He laments that the specter of communism has greatly influenced contemporary politics. Thanks to communism, Eastern Europe is in many ways forty years behind the West. A desire to keep up with the West at all costs has caused rampant corruption in all levels of government.

In recent decades, the Church has suffered from a malaise, too. The purifying fire of communism produced zealous Catholics ready to sacrifice and die for the Faith. But the era of liberalism has produced lackadaisical laity, culturally Catholic but lacking deeper engagement.

Mikloško reflects:

> Even the Catholic Church in Slovakia is still looking for its identity. The idea that Slovakia is a Catholic country because 60 percent of the population identifies as Catholic is a myth. That 60 percent is disappearing. Slovakia is slowly becoming a secular, consumerist country, and the Church will have to find a way to operate in it. Thirty years of freedom shows what we really are, and the reality is that there is a kind of spiritual helplessness without a deeper vision. I personally see it as a great challenge for the Church to bring this spiritual dimension and hope back into society.

The Church has again become silent—in a different, more subtle way.

Memorialization

As the blood of martyrs is the seed of the Church, knowledge and education *about* these martyrs can serve to reinvigorate a directionless faith.

In this vein, Mikloško is a great supporter of memorializing the nation's suffering and resilience under communism. For such recent history, there is still a great deal of work to be done.

Synthesizing the communist period into Slovaks' collective memory is "not an easy problem," he writes, "especially when the descendants of the communists of that time are still alive and have representation in the media, education, and politics." He is encouraged that Slovakia has begun to come to terms with the Tiso era and its part in the Holocaust, but recognizes there is a

long way to go in reckoning with the complex, prolonged period of communism.

Some measurable progress has been made. In the past thirty years, hundreds of local plaques and monuments have been erected to the Czechoslovak victims of communism. The Institute of National Memory, which interprets both the Nazi and communist eras, was founded in 2003. The Museum of the Victims of Communism in Košice was just established in 2021, featuring multimedia exhibits and archives of oral histories, photographs, and documents. Its goal is to provide education and open dialogue on a previously ignored, almost taboo subject.

Founded by Pavol Hric, a Košice native who worked with the secret Church, its repository includes pages on the secret Church and religious persecution at large.[71] The museum's website recognizes the sacrifice of those who "were able to endure the inevitable suffering bravely, remained faithful to the truth and did not succumb to the lies, lies that often accused them of absurd things." A crucial aspect of the museum's work is providing educational resources for schools. Mikloško also identifies the school system as the next frontier.

The lessons of communism are as universal as the testaments of the saints. I asked Mikloško what lessons he believes readers of an American Catholic publisher should take from his testimony.

> There are many totalitarianisms in the world: ideological, military, and police, but also media, economic, and social. Against all these totalitarianisms, the individual, the human individual, is faced with the decision of how to approach them. Will he adapt and perhaps benefit from it, or will he remain internally free and be willing to suffer for this freedom?
>
> Our experience is that a person, in addition to deciding to be himself, must not remain lonely. In addition to faith in God, we were saved by small communities in which we felt accepted by others, also confronted in our opinions, whether we were falling into self-deception, and at the same time encouraged that we were not alone, that we had friends with us who were willing to help us. Just like us, we felt the need to help our friends.[72]

[71] Múzeum Obetí Komunizmu (Museum of Victims of Communism), https://mok.sk/kategorie_obeti/tajna-cirkev/.

[72] The West's struggle against "soft totalitarianism" and the lessons it can learn from Czechoslovak anti-communist resistance are the topics of Rod Dreher's book *Live Not by Lies: A Manual for Christian Dissidents* (New York: Sentinel, 2020).

"That's our experience of communism," he continues. "I think that a similar experience awaits people in America, when in many situations in life they will feel that their personality and inner integrity have been touched, and they will have to make a decision."

No matter what particular machinations of the enemy we face, we have countless examples of heroic virtue in the *Ecclesia Silentii* of Czechoslovakia, once-silent witnesses who have finally found their voice.

Olga Koutna-Izzo

"I was born in a family that was Catholic on both sides, and I never left the Church. This would promise rather a boring story were it not for the fact that I was born in Czechoslovakia just three weeks before the Communist takeover."

Olga was born in 1948 in the Czech city of Brno. Largely isolated from the early horrors of communism in her happy home, she had a warm, comfortable childhood surrounded by her loving parents and two older sisters. Every Sunday, the family would walk the two miles to Mass at a beautiful baroque-era church. She remembers her parents' admonitions to tread carefully so as not to dirty their Sunday clothes. In the controlled economy, children's clothes were hard to come by: the stores were stocked once per week, but the best merchandise was stashed away by the owners, to be used as barter with their influential acquaintances. In fact, most of the stores were completely empty. The trade gridlock meant the absence of any new technology, which meant that the washing machine was still just an unattainable dream. Since all laundry was done by hand, adding to the daily workload, and clothes were such precious commodities, a simple walk could become a minefield.

The grand utopian economy was proving itself to be a cruel joke, saddling its inhabitants with work and worry.

Nevertheless, these Sunday walks to Mass were one of Olga's favorite events of the week. She quickly became enamored of the solemnity of the Mass, the intricate and mysterious Latin language—this was before Vatican II—and the stunning architecture. She enjoyed memorizing parts of the propers and credits these early experiences with fostering her love of languages (she would go on to study and teach Latin as part of a classical Catholic curriculum).

As Olga embarked on her school years, everything seemed normal. As previously mentioned, parochial schools were not common in Czechoslovakia, and religious education was not a regular part of the curriculum. Olga's school still offered religion classes as a noncredit option, and about half the elementary school students chose to enroll. There was certainly no shortage of material: the region's illustrious and sometimes tumultuous religious history meant that walking through the streets was an education in itself. Brno boasts of at least a half dozen major Catholic churches dating from the Middle Ages.

One year, in either the third or fourth grade, this religious instruction came to an abrupt end. Waiting with other students outside the religious ed classroom, Olga noticed the leader of the Young Pioneers sidle up to the group and demand to know why they were there.

The Young Pioneers was a communist youth club designed to indoctrinate children with socialist principles and prime them to one day enter the Communist Party. It served as a counterpart to the Hitler Youth movement in its cult-like worship of totalitarian leaders, its exclusivity, and the demands it placed on its members. Even as the Boy Scouts flourished in the United States, twentieth-century Europe abounded with youth movements, often focused on fitness, survivalism, and health. Since 1862, the Czechs had prided themselves on their popular *Sokol* movement, a youth gymnastics organization named for the national symbol, the falcon. This cultural tradition was craftily hijacked by communist ideologues, who poisoned any healthy outlet with their pernicious doctrine. Olga was pressured to join the Young Pioneers, but she knew from the start she wanted nothing to do with them. Olga describes this particular Pioneer leader as not very bright, an unthinking drone of the system. Such people kept the communist system humming steadily along.

As Caryll Houselander has argued in her psychological expedition *Guilt*, personal identification with a totalizing group—such as a cult or a totalitarian system—is often a result of an inner lack of conviction, a confused identity, or an unresolved guilty conscience. The many eager collaborators and petty tyrants who used the excuse "just following orders" when convenient (yet wielded outsized power when it pleased them) formed the base mechanism of control under communism. Their buy-in to the system consisted not in transcendent belief in communist doctrine but in the shared, self-congratulating pride of demons. Luxuriating in their own perceived influence, they become torturers in a million small ways. Anyone who has dealt with a TSA agent on a power trip has been given a revealing glimpse into the type of personality that thrived under communism.

The historian Christopher Browning has furnished a fascinating analysis of the human capacity for brutality in his study *Ordinary Men*, which profiles members of the Nazi *Einsatzgruppen*, an elite SS division responsible for shooting thousands of Jews on the eastern front. The members of this division had been ordinary (even *boring*) professionals just years before. Accountants, lawyers, and family men had been transformed, in a matter of months, into callous, sadistic killers. Browning concludes, in a thesis reminiscent of Joseph Conrad's *Heart of Darkness*, that morality is largely situational. These men were placed in a situation where killing was the norm—where murder was expected, even encouraged. Seemingly unencumbered by a strong religious or moral foundation, they simply adapted to the status quo.

The disturbing conclusion is that humans, when unfettered by objective religious morality, will take the opportunity to brutalize their fellow man *because they can*. It's that simple. Under communism, where objective Christian morality was officially abolished, how could there be any other way of operating? Instead of cooperation and community, there was only exploitation, every man for himself. Far from its purported doctrine of fraternal love, communism fostered only further isolation and atomization. Becoming a selfish, petty tyrant was the natural conclusion to the subverted moral order. This is one of the many reasons why devout Catholics, whose morality is objective, eternal, and nonnegotiable, were such thorns in the side of communists. Not only did they refuse to go along with the overall ideological program, but they refused to play the game even for personal gain. They rejected worldly gain outright, choosing to save their souls instead. Such people cannot be manipulated. But people of weak faith—or no faith—can, and were thus prime targets for the creation of the new communist phenotype. Those with selfish, worldly ambitions would find these prideful desires courted by communists, who would silently take their souls in return.

Back to the petty tyrant in question—the first of many such bureaucratic personalities that Olga would encounter in her life. The Young Pioneer leader approached the group with a phony smile and, in a nosy manner, demanded to know what they were doing. The students naively revealed that they were waiting for their religion class to begin.

Immediately, the teacher launched into a furious tirade. "Don't you know that our society is atheist? That religion is the opium of the people? Who authorized this class?!"

Her screed sounded like the latest canned missive from *Pravda*. Olga is convinced the woman cannot have even known what opium is: it was well known that she had gained her teaching position not because of any academic credentials, but simply because she was an enthusiastic member of the Communist Party. Parroting the party line, using words she didn't understand … Did she even know what she believed? In any case, this meddling teacher managed to get the principal fired for allowing these religious classes. Needless to say, that marked the end of religious education at the school.

It was around this time — the middle of the 1950s — that Olga began to take more notice of what was going on in the outside world. She particularly remembers one late October afternoon. She was playing at a friend's house. Her friend's mother was preparing dinner in the kitchen while listening to the radio. Olga was intrigued: her family did not have a radio at home. Her parents had made this decision to protect their daughters as much as possible from the onslaught of communist propaganda. The worst fate under communism — worse than imprisonment or death — would be to lose your soul. To lose the psychological battle, lose touch with reality, to win the victory over oneself and learn to love Big Brother.

This radio broadcast didn't sound like the routine propaganda hour, however. Olga inched closer to the kitchen, riveted by the announcer's voice, which was choking with emotion. The announcer's crocodile tears proved to be a next-level propaganda move, an emotional manipulation tactic. He was beside himself with outrage against those "evil" counterrevolutionaries in Hungary who tried to overthrow their wonderful communist government. It was that fateful day in 1956, when Soviet tanks rolled into Budapest.

When she returned home in the evening, her parents were talking about some Cardinal Mindszenty, his imprisonment, and his asylum at the U.S. Mission in Budapest. Could other countries really be in the same situation? Who was this heroic Catholic, this prince of the Church, and why did the communists hate him so much?

✠ ✠ ✠

Soon enough, the Koutna family would experience this hallmark anti-Catholicism closer to home.

Some time later, Olga's father, who was a professor of chemistry on the veterinary faculty of the University of Brno, applied for promotion to associate professor. The promotion committee, composed of members of the Communist Party, refused to recommend his promotion because he continued to attend Mass—and even took his family with him! He was failing miserably in his duty to promote "the atheistic worldview," as was required from all educators. The committee made it known that he was lucky to be allowed to stay and teach, even if he never got tenure. He was allowed to publish his articles only because they were co-signed by a communist colleague (who thereby received the credit of co-authorship even though he had taken no part whatsoever in either research or writing).

A few years later Olga's older sisters finished grade eight and applied to go to high school. Admission to a high school was a very selective process, but good grades were not the main criterion for being admitted: the student's "social" background played a more important, in fact, crucial role. Children from so-called "working families" (in truth, from Communist families) were almost automatically assured of acceptance regardless of their grades, but those from the wrong families—and Catholics were the worst of the worst—had only slim chances of being accepted. The applications of both sisters were first rejected, and they were admitted only on appeal, after their father wrote to the minister of education. About the same time, the family's church attendance was starting to cause problems for her father at school. The family decided to forgo their beloved home parish and go to churches in different parts of Brno—one weekend here, the next across the city—to avoid being seen by people from her father's school.

Schools were under tremendous pressure to weed out the so-called "religious elements" among their ranks. The communists could not afford to have Catholic teachers polluting the minds of the next generation of communist leaders—the first generation to be raised completely atheist. Principals and department chairmen would send designated spies to wait outside churches and write down the names of teachers from their schools who were not yet "reeducated." The delinquent teachers were then given a choice: stop attending Mass or find their names on a blacklist.

It was then that the family began investigating options for secret Mass attendance. Olga recalls the uncertainty and secrecy that her family was forced into:

> No wonder that in such conditions religious life had to be secret: no meetings, no common meals, parties, none of the usual activities found in parishes here. We went to Mass at dawn or at dusk and then hurried home. We didn't know, and didn't want to know, the people who were at Mass with us, and didn't want them to know us. If interrogated, we could say with a clear conscience that we didn't know them. We lived in an atmosphere of constant uncertainty and suspicion: Are our neighbors, or the parents of our

classmates, collaborators of the secret police? If so, will they inform on us?

Another challenge that the family faced was the uncertainty of the priests' allegiance. We have already discussed the "juring priests" of the national church, who swore fealty to the communist state rather than the Vatican. For clergy, it was a clear-cut choice. To remain Catholic, priests had to resist this temptation to collaborate. For the laity, however, it was a more complicated matter. Sometimes it was not clear what the priests believed. Sometimes priests would collaborate with the government on certain occasions, or to certain degrees, but not entirely. They would share different opinions with different people. They would have one story for the secret police, and another for their congregation. Who could be trusted? But every week, Sunday would arrive, and it would be time to fulfill your Sunday obligation. These questions faded into the background as the utmost importance of the sacraments took precedence. How much vetting could the laity realistically be expected to do before attending Mass? Receiving the sacraments, being flooded with these graces — was that not the priority?

In Olga's life, the greatest challenge posed by questionable collaborator clergy was in the Sacrament of Confession. It was well known in Brno that priests loyal to the government, or under tremendous pressure, would sometimes break the seal of Confession, turning penitents in to the secret police. This horrific violation of Church law (which incurs an automatic excommunication) had become commonplace. In addition to the spiritual risks of associating with such juring priests, the laity also faced these political and safety risks. Olga's solution was to go from church to church for Confession, much as her family did for Mass. She tried to be as unassuming as possible, and spoke quietly in the confessional, hoping to remain anonymous.

The shortage of bishops also posed a problem for Olga's sacramental life. As we have discussed, many bishops were imprisoned, and the secret bishops (such as Ján Korec) who were consecrated under the Secret Mandates were spread thin in their apostolate. Confirmation was a particularly difficult sacrament to receive, as ordinations and consecrations were more urgent in the emergency situation. Sometimes, bishops from neighboring countries would secretly cross the border. Then-Bishop Karol Wojtyła is reported to have crossed the Tatra Mountains to administer the Sacrament of Confirmation in the region of Slovakia adjacent to the Polish border.

But such prospects were few and far between. Olga never had the chance to be confirmed. Nevertheless, the Holy Spirit was clearly active in her life, supplying His gifts of knowledge, fortitude, and fear of the Lord for the trials to come. To this day, she has not received the sacrament. The maleffects of communism remain long after the regime.

✠ ✠ ✠

Exercising basic religious freedom now amounted to a daily struggle, where the faithful had to creatively war-game their every move. The stress from this extreme duress built up. During Olga's second to last year of middle school, her father suddenly passed away at the age of fifty-seven. Olga knows that all the years of harassment, fear, uncertainty, cruelty, and hopelessness under communism took their toll on her father's health. She wishes that he could have lived to see the collapse of the regime that so persecuted him.

In 1963, it was Olga's turn to finish middle school and apply for admission to high school. There was no one to appeal to the minister on her behalf, as her father had done for her sisters. Yet, to her great surprise, she was admitted immediately, with no need for an appeal.

After completing high school, she applied for admission to the University of Brno to study classics, Latin and French. Again, she was admitted without problems. She attributed this to her high GPA and to the fact that in the sixties, during the period of "normalization," the political situation had somewhat improved.

It was only many years later that she learned the real reason she was allowed to study. A neighbor, who was a member of the Communist Street Committee that, among other things, recommended or rejected applications for secondary and post-secondary schools, eventually told her the truth. On the evening of the committee meeting where Olga's application to high school was supposed to be discussed, the neighbor didn't feel well and intended to skip the meeting. But at the last moment, he decided to go after all. The chairman of the committee read her application and automatically decided that the youngest child of a family known to be practicing Catholics would definitely not be recommended. But the neighbor stood up and vehemently defended Olga and her family. His arguments must have been so persuasive that the rest of the committee members finally agreed with him, and so her application to go to high school was approved. The same situation repeated itself three years later when Olga applied for the university. The same neighbor *again* intervened in her favor and prevailed. Thus, she was allowed to study, determining the course of the rest of her life. Her entire fate was decided by the whims of one bureaucrat, his moment of conscience, and his suddenly restored health. The communist system was as capricious as the wind.

While luck sometimes favored the talented, this arbitrary nepotism of communism would have disastrous effects in the quality of all industries and sectors, from the factory to the army, as evidenced by the unqualified Young Pioneer leader from Olga's elementary school. Officially, students were told that only those with the highest GPA would be allowed to pursue higher studies, but in reality your fate depended on the arbitrary whims of the apparatchiks. Everyone knew the official story was a lie, but they were powerless to effect any institutional change.

This one small account, often attributed to Aleksandr Solzhenitsyn or to writer Elena Gokhorova, exemplifies the Soviet psychological tongue twister which perfectly encapsulates the intricate lies and mind-games of communism, from the schools to the gulags:

We know they are lying.
They know they are lying.
They know that we know they are lying.
We know that they know we know they are lying.
And still they continue to lie.
And still we pretend to believe them.

✠ ✠ ✠

Olga's first two years at the university were quite exciting. The atmosphere of the city, the novelty of being surrounded by scholars, the chance to study topics that fascinated her—it was an exhilarating experience.

Yet communism presented more challenges than a simple barrier to admission. After years of communist control of institutions, the curriculum was poisoned with rewritten history, sham economics, and an overbearing ideological overtone. In short, all students were subjected to attempted indoctrination. Olga would soon learn that classes in "political science" were part of the core curriculum. In reality, this meant a core instruction in Communist Party doctrine. The syllabus could be interpreted as follows:

> *Politics = Marxism*
>
> *Economics = communism*
>
> *Social studies = atheism*

Despite the mandatory propaganda courses, Olga noticed that there was a general mood of free expression among the professors. In contrast to the regimented regurgitation of the party line she had suffered through in elementary school, the college professors were not afraid to speak their minds, even when they held dissident opinions. Some went so far as to criticize the government or the Communist Party outright—an unfathomable offense.

Emboldened by the professors' outspokenness, Olga commenced going to church without fear of being denounced or expelled from the university. The general softening of restrictions was a harbinger of the official relaxation of the Prague Spring.

Olga speaks fondly of this hopeful period:

> And then came the glorious spring of 1968!
>
> For a few short months life was like a dream. Imagine
> that after long years you finally left a very cold and dark
> cave and came into sunshine. For several months the Com-
> munists were on the defensive. Journalists could write freely
> and without censorship. And how they took advantage
> of this opportunity! Articles began to appear describing
> what was really going on in the fifties. People who spent
> years in prison came forward with their stories. And their
> stories were shocking. That kind of stories one used to hear
> from the Nazi concentration camp survivors. How could
> this happen in our "enlightened" society, where everyone
> would get according to his needs, where "exploitation" was
> eliminated, where the new socialist man was supposed to
> replace the old selfish and greedy "capitalist," where people

would just hold hands and sing kumbaya or some other
socialism building song and baked pigeons would fly right
into their mouths?

A hopeful mood infected the city of Brno. Olga remembers that
strangers would even smile again at each other and joke in the streets.
The Catholic churches were full again, especially with young people.
Olga vividly remembers Easter of that year, when she got to
meet a living martyr of the underground Church. For the first time
since the initial anti-Catholic repressions of 1948–1950, the bishop
of Brno, Karel Skoupý, was allowed to celebrate the Easter Mass.
As a bishop, Skoupý had been arrested soon after the 1948 coup.
Bishop Skoupý had been in prison for fifteen years, interned at an
undisclosed location and unable to exercise his episcopal function
or communicate with the outside world. He was amnestied in the
period of "normalization" in 1968. After his death in 1972, tens of
thousands of mourners came to his funeral. The communist government, returning to its ways of oppression after the Soviet invasion,
prevented the appointment of a successor bishop until 1990.[73] Brno
would again be left without a shepherd.

For now, though, Bishop Skoupý's triumphant return to Brno
marked a great victory for the repressed Catholics of the city. The
historic cathedral of Sts. Peter and Paul, a national icon dating from
the eleventh century, was completely full, with hundreds more faithful spilling out onto the sidewalk.

After Mass, the bishop went down the aisle delivering a blessing.
Olga was only a few feet from him. She describes his prematurely

---

haggard appearance, his health stolen by years in prison. He walked only with difficulty, but smiled kindly.

✠ ✠ ✠

Spurred by the Easter hope of 1968, Olga planned to spend the next Easter in Rome. Travel restrictions were lifted during the Prague Spring; such basic freedom, unimaginable just years before, was now possible. Rather than sneak from church to church, eyes downcast, she could now triumphantly visit the beating heart of the Catholic Faith—and maybe even see the pope himself!

The economic deprivation of communism was not so easily remedied, however. Olga knew that she had to save up a few months' salary from her after-school jobs to be able to afford a decent coat for the trip. She also knew she'd have to put a little extra aside to bribe the shopkeeper to save it for her. Despite these challenges, the future was filled with hope.

The beautiful Springtime of Prague was as delicate and short-lived as the new blooms. "All our hope came crashing down on August 21, 1968," Olga laments. "Back to the cold, dark, cruel cave." The sickle swung back into place as Soviet tanks rolled into Prague.

On that fateful day, when František Mikloško's physics professor threw up his hands in Bratislava, Olga was in the heart of Brno.

At 6:00 a.m., the family's phone rang, and Olga's mother answered. It was one of her friends calling to inform them that the worst had happened: their country had been invaded by the Soviet army, exactly as they had feared might happen.

"Shock. Anger. Horror," is the way Olga describes it. They immediately turned on the radio. The announcers were urging people to stay calm. They also suggested that people do their best to appease the Russian soldiers. They told them to go outside and talk to the Russian soldiers, to try and convince them that there was no counterrevolution in Czechoslovakia. This was truly a desperate measure. How could this groveling ever work? Needless to say, no one from the household took the announcers up on this sycophantic proposition.

In the afternoon, Olga ventured downtown with her brother-in-law to see if any stores were open so they could buy food. There was no public transportation that day; Brno was like a ghost town. As they were walking back, they saw a group of forty people standing around a Soviet tank. It was only three blocks from their house.

Standing on top of the tank was a young man Olga recognized as a former high school classmate, whom she remembers as "a hugely enthusiastic Pioneer Youth member and an aspiring commie." He was putting on a great show of deference to the Soviet soldiers, gesticulating wildly, explaining to the soldiers that their trip was useless. *Of course* there is no counterrevolution in our country. Czechoslovakia is full of loyal citizens, can't you see? You might as well turn back now, comrades!

Olga and her brother-in-law approached the group and watched the whole scene play out. After several minutes of the communist striver's comical performance, the Soviet tank commander had had enough. The soldiers brusquely ordered him to go away, along with his gallery of equally ridiculous supporters and the other, less friendly elements in the crowd.

Nobody obeyed.

The soldier repeated his order. The crowd stood its ground.

Refusing to try a third time, he barked an order to a young, blonde soldier. The boy soldier aimed the gun of the massive tank directly into the crowd.

This time, it worked. The group dispersed, running frantically in all directions. Olga observed from their facial expressions that they were suddenly compelled to make a series of mental calculations: How would they make excuses for having been part of this group? What would they tell their boss? How soon could they open their case for rehabilitation with the party? What did "freedom" matter, anyway?

The hypocrisy enraged her. These people, who had just minutes before been putting on a great show of courage, were suddenly reduced to desperate, cowardly conformists.

But the Russian soldier, daring to give orders to her countrymen, in her homeland, almost enraged her more.

The most depressing fact was that this show of resistance, however minuscule and polluted by the groveling of a party member, would all be in vain. It only took one threat from the cold steel of the Soviet military to damn the country back to the "ugly, cold, cruel cave where a human life didn't mean much."

The moment was slipping away. The hopes of the Prague Spring were relegated back to the realm of dreams, reflected in the crestfallen faces of the scattered neighbors.

It was all too much. And so, Olga lost her temper: "Utterly. Totally. Completely."

With the crowd dispersed, there was a clear path up to the tank. As if watching herself in a dream, Olga realized she was marching closer to the tank, yelling: "This is *my* country, *my* city, *my* street, and I will not listen to any order coming from you!"

Minutes passed as she continued to upbraid the soldiers, daring to look right into the eye of the commander. The commander, yet again, gave an order to the blonde soldier. Again, the boy maneuvered the large gun of the tank. But this time, it was pointed just at Olga.

Reality catching up to her, Olga lost her train of thought. She was staring into a four-inch-diameter gun that could take her head off there and then. She tried pushing it away, to no avail. She could no longer even see the soldiers or the tank behind it; everything melted away into the black hole of the gun barrel.

Yet she still didn't move. She remembers thinking, "They will have to shoot me because I am not running away." She had witnessed courage. Hadn't she met Bishop Skoupý just a few months before? Maybe this was her time to sacrifice.

The commander nodded to the boy. Incredulous, with a white face and tears in his eyes, he slowly put his finger on the trigger. She still didn't move. "In fact, what was going through my head was this: so, this is it, I wonder how it will look on the other side."

But God had different plans for Olga's life.

A hysterical scream interrupted her musings: a woman's voice calling her name, using the diminutive, familiar form that only people who loved her would use. The woman grabbed her left arm and jerked her away, out of the line of fire. She was sobbing, repeating that the Russians were not worth it, begging Olga to go with her.

As Olga came to her senses, she recognized her mother's friend, the one who had called in the morning to warn about the invasion. "My guardian angel."

As she turned away from the tank, she saw that she had an audience: all of the people from the small group had watched the scene, standing at a safe distance, frozen, with horror on their faces. Olga wanted to yell at them and ask why they had been so cowardly, why they hadn't helped her.

She didn't get the chance, as her friend prudently hauled her away and walked her home. She even waited until Olga had gone inside and closed the door, just to be sure she wouldn't attempt to run back out and repeat the incident.

Olga was safe to fight another day.

She and her mother's friend had a tacit agreement not to talk about the episode. Olga never told her family, and the friend kept her lips sealed. Only many years later did Olga feel ready to talk about this event, when she briefly mentioned it to some of her students. Finally, in 2018, for the fiftieth anniversary of the invasion of Czechoslovakia, she told her sister. And now, she tells the world about her encounter with the Russian tank, a one-woman army arrayed against the whole of Soviet totalitarianism.

Olga does not think of her actions that day as any sort of heroic resistance:

> Mine was not an act of bravery but rather of desperately and foolishly maintaining a piece of my human dignity, knowing that everything would again be taken away from me. The only thing I could do at that moment was scream and say that I was not afraid of them, I would not run, I would never give up.

✠ ✠ ✠

But preserving that God-given dignity is the most fundamental act of resistance anyone can perform. Writer and historian Joachim Fest, who suffered under the Nazi empire, writes that holding on to your soul is the bedrock of all meaningful resistance.

Joachim grew up in a strong Catholic family, which suffered similar kinds of white martyrdom for its refusal to adopt the perverse ideology of a bloodthirsty regime. His father lost his job, he had to flee forced conscription, education became a nightmare. They simply lived as Catholics at a time when doing so was not fashionable, not acceptable.

Fest expresses a sentiment very similar to Olga's opening line in this chapter: "We had the dubious advantage of remaining exactly who we had always been, and so of once again being the odd ones out."

Fest's memoir *Not I: Memoirs of a German Childhood* portrays a story of heroic mental and spiritual resistance to tyranny. Such resistance cannot always be measured in *samizdat* texts, years in prison, or physical scars. Just as Olga's family avoided the radio to protect the minds of their daughters, Fest writes that his father's resistance consisted of protecting the souls in his care from succumbing to the propaganda:

> Apart from helping out in a small way a few times, he hadn't been able to do anything; his main concern had been to keep the totalitarian infection from affecting his family and one or two friends. When it came to the Nazis, as he had often observed, even the passing thought of giving in had been enough and a person was already lost.[74]

The major battle to be won was against oneself: one's own weakness, temptations, and fears. Not caving in, not becoming one of them … that is a victory! Acknowledging reality … that too is a victory! Preserving your eternal soul … that is the only victory that matters.

As an atheist, anti-Catholic regime, communism's goal is not just to kill the body, but to murder souls. Coercion and temptation, impossible choices, brainwashing: these all seek to take souls away from God. When viewed from eternity, there are many fates worse than death: collaborating, giving in, giving up the Faith, downplaying the Faith, committing sin. So, maintaining free will, dignity, and untarnished Catholic principles is the greatest form of mental resistance.

---

[74] Joachim Fest, *Not I: Memoirs of a German Childhood* (New York: Other Press, 2014), 359.

Decades after these events have taken place, as communism is slowly disappearing from the collective consciousness, this intellectual, spiritual resistance remains as relevant as ever. The Faith, and the principles that follow, are eternal.

Fest notes that it was Pontius Pilate's existential question "What is truth?" that motivated him to write down his story. We know that Truth is ultimately a Person.

As with so many witnesses to tyranny, simply preserving the truth, writing it down, is enough — it will speak for itself. As St. Augustine purportedly said, "The truth is like a lion; you don't have to defend it. Let it loose; it will defend itself."

The witnesses continue to resist evil by telling their stories. They inoculate future generations from falling for the same lies.

✠ ✠ ✠

After the drama of 1968, it seemed the world would end. But life continued. Solzhenitsyn has described the U.S.S.R. as a whole as the *bolshaya zona* — the "big zone," an extension of the microcosm of the Gulag. In Czechoslovakia, many of the same elements would coalesce to add to the feeling that the country was, yet again, an open-air prison.

Fearing new repressions and hardships, thousands of people fled to the West. Olga's older sister, along with her husband and family, were among them. Olga stayed in Brno to continue with her studies. In September 1968, she started her third year at the university. At first, things seemed to be as they were before the invasion: professors and students continued to be outspoken, and yet were not expelled. But by the spring of 1971, the old constricting, repressive atmosphere returned.

Entering her final semester, Olga was preoccupied with her thesis, preparing for final oral exams, and making plans for a study year abroad in France. Two weeks before her final exams, she received a letter from the dean informing her that her scholarship to study in France was revoked, effective immediately. The reason? She was a bad citizen of the Czechoslovak Socialist Republic. She had still refused to join the Youth Organization, the college-level iteration of the Young Pioneers. Furthermore, she had a sister "illegally" residing in Canada. (All political refugees and others who fled Czechoslovakia for the West were considered to have betrayed the state). They probably feared Olga would stay in France—or worse, import Western ideals back into Czechoslovakia.

The university allowed her to quickly complete her bachelor's degree, but then sent her abruptly on her way. Thrown back out into the world, the next hurdle to overcome was finding a job. Olga wanted to be a teacher, but given her experiences in the school system to this point, she knew it wasn't going to be easy. She already had black marks against her for her Catholic Faith and her refusal to join the Communist Party, but the added strike of a sister abroad now meant she was among the lowest of the low. One superintendent, after reviewing Olga's file, told her that she was "absolutely useless to our socialist society."

She finally found a teaching position at a high school in a small town in southern Bohemia. But it didn't take long before she ran into trouble here, too.

Since she turned twenty-two, Olga had worn a small golden cross, a birthday present from her oldest sister. Wearing a cross was a serious offense in the eyes of the principal. He ordered her to stop wearing it to classes. Craftily using the communists' own words against them, she replied that the Czech constitution guaranteed the right to religious freedom, and therefore his request was unconstitutional. While the constitution technically did protect religious freedom, in practice it had always been a lie. The purpose of this provision was mainly to keep up a facade of "democracy" to the outside world. Communists always claimed to be the true heirs of democracy. In their minds, religious freedom was more accurately defined as freedom *from* religion, anyway.

The principal exploded at this response and railed that the constitution was "just a piece of paper" and shouldn't be taken seriously.

✠ ✠ ✠

Olga moved on to a teaching position at another high school but kept encountering the same problems and personalities. At her next school, the principal had decided that young professors on the staff should form a Communist Youth Organization cell. The minimal number for starting a chapter was five. They had four teachers on board already; Olga would have made five. But of course she would not join.

She refused on the pretext that, at almost thirty years old, she was too old to qualify. "Oh no," the principal assured her, " 'Young' extends to the age of thirty-five!" Robbed of this easy out, she simply refused to join.

Olga thinks back to how this decision impacted her life: "My life would have been so much easier if I had joined that stupid organization, but I simply couldn't. It would have been like selling my soul to the devil. Not a good bargain. And so, I continued enduring the daily small chicaneries and bullying by the principal. Death by a thousand cuts."

Life continued in this vein throughout the seventies. Two more memorable events characterized the decade.

The first was October 16, 1978. Polish Cardinal Karol Wojtyła was elected pope. Olga heard the news on the radio late in the afternoon that day, and felt deep down that the days of the evil empire were numbered. It was only a matter of time.

Then, two years later, when an opportunity presented itself, she officially defected from Czechoslovakia. She joined her sister in Canada, where she was able to resume her studies and earn a doctorate. She got married and moved with her husband to the United States, settling in Michigan. In 1999, just one year after its foundation, she joined the faculty of Ave Maria College. What a difference, to be at a Catholic college! She marvels: "Finally, I could teach at a place where I didn't have to hide my golden cross nor sneak into church at dawn or dusk."

Olga's story has a happy ending. She persevered through the trials of communism, and eventually escaped them. Her country was delivered.

"Compared to some, mine is not a very interesting story," she reflects. "Nobody in my immediate family spent long years in prison. (My only claim to some drama is that I almost got shot on August 21, 1968.) We lived that unhappy, shabby, hopeless life like millions of other families in Czechoslovakia."

The "ordinariness" of Olga's story makes it that much more relatable to Catholics today. The white martyrdom she suffered—a million small temptations to compromise, "death by a thousand cuts"—mirrors the challenges that Catholics will most likely face in the secularist political environment of the twenty-first century. Olga reminds us that to keep the Faith is the greatest victory:

> Thinking back over my youth, I am very grateful to my parents for having the courage to bring their children up in faith and for never leaving the Church in spite of the terrible danger it presented. It was faith that helped us survive and gave us hope in those dark, cruel years. It is really simple: all you need is faith, humility, and courage. "Yea, though I walk through the valley of the shadow of death, I will fear no evil: for thou art with me; thy rod and thy staff they comfort me" (Ps. 23:4).

Czechoslovak Conclusion

"One ear turned toward Heaven and the other to the Lubyanka." With these words, Aleksandr Solzhenitsyn describes collaborator priests of the Russian Orthodox Church who informed on their congregation, condemning many to arrest and interrogation at the feared Lubyanka Prison in Moscow.

Yet I've always held on to this image as a representation of the martyrs of communism. They are aware that keeping eyes on Heaven will, inevitably, lead them to the Lubyanka in one way or another. There is no Easter without Good Friday. Heaven is not opened to us until the consummation of the Passion.

For many Catholics living in those impossible times, when the simple act of being a baptized Catholic was illegal, there was no Heaven without the Lubyanka. It became the means of sanctification.

This double meaning truly analogizes the two ultimate courses of action available to citizens of communist Czechoslovakia: collaborate or die. The swaths of gray area between these two fates comprised the daily balancing act, in a million decisions, of those who knew that holding onto your life is secondary to saving your soul.

Orlando Figes, in his study of the social effects of informant culture in the U.S.S.R., identifies two types of "whisperer": the person who whispers so as not to be heard, and the person who whispers secrets about others. But perhaps there is a third kind of whisperer: one who quietly but firmly states the truth to anyone who will listen.

The Heaven-Lubyanka double entendre provides an interesting framework for the forces at play among Czechoslovak Catholics.

On the one hand, the national church: The Potemkin lie, a state operation with the facade of Catholicism. Informant priests, doctrinally compromised, in worldly positions, legal and accepted by the state but in schism from the Vicar of Christ on earth.

On the other, the unadulterated Catholic Faith: membership in the Mystical Body of Christ, now hectic and underground, shrouded by the constant threat of arrest, torture, imprisonment, martyrdom. In between: all sorts of characters to be assessed, trusted, distrusted, and ultimately evangelized and saved. Many false starts or incomplete truths. And at the most basic level, your own divided heart, surrounded by temptation and uncertainty.

Catholicism and communism are unassimilable ideologies. All attempts to assimilate the Church with communism fail: it is as impossible a task as integrating Heaven and Hell.

Balancing these two competing worldviews required citizens to always keep one ear turned toward Heaven and the other to the Lubyanka. Catholics were forced to thread the needle in increasingly complicated ways just to survive and keep the Faith alive.

The only way *to* Heaven was *through* the Lubyanka, that particular iteration of this vale of tears.

Just as the cross, a symbol of Roman execution, is transformed into the means of our salvation, so too are saints pictured with the instruments of their martyrdom. St. Catherine of Alexandria leans on her wheel; St. Lawrence is pictured with his grill.

The hammer and sickle will always be symbols of oppression, atheism, human rights abuses, and societal destruction. But they were also the ultimate means of sanctification for millions of Catholics whose faith was tested. In Czechoslovakia, the collapse of communism vindicated the heroes of the secret Church in a direct, observable way. When the glories of the utopian state disappeared, the shredded tatters of the Church remained.

Anywhere the hammer and sickle triumphed, the Church confounded the worldly victory for the salvation of souls.

CHAPTER FOUR

Hungary and Romania

ADA NEMES BAN was born in the small Transylvanian town of Marosvásárhely/Târgu Mureş (Hungarian/Romanian) in 1982. Although she left with her family for the United States in 1989, her communist childhood has made a lasting impression. She is of 100 percent Hungarian descent, but her town had changed hands several times over the centuries, most recently being ceded to Romania after the First World War. The two countries' borders would undergo more paroxysms after World War II. Ada's family was placed squarely under the tutelage of the Socialist Republic of Romania, the longest-lasting European communist state.

The preposterous cult of personality around Nicolae Ceauşescu rivals that of any other dictator. The hyperbolic expressions of power would have made him a clownish figure, if not for the power he wielded over life and death. Known for his brutal policies, luxurious lifestyle, and severe censorship and repression, his televised execution was celebrated across the world.

Romania had become communist in 1947, after the country's attempt at a separate peace with the United States failed and it fell under the Soviet sphere of influence. Like Czechoslovakia, Romania followed a Soviet path of anti-religious measures, complete with expulsion or imprisonment of priests, seizure and consolidation of Church property, and repression of the sacraments and public worship.

Ada's family experienced persecution for being a Hungarian minority in newly Romanian lands, too. The Ceaușescu regime used ethnic discrimination to divide and control the populace.

By the time Ada was growing up, the citizens had become completely disillusioned by Ceaușescu. "Everyone hated him," she remembers. Her parents, as Olga's had with the radio, refused to keep a TV in the house so as to shield their children from propaganda as much as possible. There was hardly anything to watch anyway: Ada remembers a ten-minute children's cartoon before bedtime, but the majority of the day was just static. The main event was Ceaușescu's daily rants: he spent an average of four hours each day addressing the people on television, lecturing on various topics and reiterating communist talking points *ad nauseum*. Ceaușescu had even gone to China on a fact-finding mission to perfect his art. It was a slow brainwashing, designed to get citizens to mentally give up. "That was the god," Ada explains, referring to the dictator. Pictures of Ceaușescu had replaced crucifixes above schoolroom doors, and citizens who didn't want trouble with the authorities would keep one in their homes, too.

Ada notes that everyone in her circle saw through his facade, simply turning off the TV and tuning him out. They knew he was a fraud, but they were powerless to do anything about it. When asked what type of resistance was available to the average person, Ada is quick to respond: "Nothing." Resistance of any kind was futile, and would only result in getting you killed. The only type of resistance was internal — maintaining sovereignty over your own mind and soul.

A small ray of light came in the form of information. The family had access to Radio Free Europe, an American-sponsored radio channel that broadcast news from a Western perspective, providing a dose of reality to those behind the Iron Curtain and emboldening them in free expression.

Ada's family had landed on the wrong side of the communist revolution in Romania. They were Hungarian. They were Christian. And they were "class enemies." Her grandparents on her father's side had been kulaks—the "rich peasants" who were specially targeted by communists everywhere. The prosperous couple raised crops with their ten children on their ancestral land.

One day, after the war, communist soldiers rolled onto their property, kicked in the door, and unceremoniously announced that the estate was being confiscated as property of the state, and that they would have to leave immediately. The family, including all ten children, were immediately forced onto the trucks. Ada's grandmother didn't even have time to put on her watch. They were resettled in a city about three hours away, in the poor-quality apartment buildings that are so emblematic of communism. In a cruel twist, they were not resettled as a family but placed in small groups wherever there were vacancies in the collective apartments. They had to find work where they could, and build up a life again. It was into this environment that Ada's father was born. Whereas his siblings had been raised in a family unit in prosperity, he was born into poverty, into a family broken down by communism.

Ada considers the emotional and spiritual toll that these events had on her grandmother to be the saddest outcome of her family's entire ordeal. Her grandmother was spiritually defeated for the rest of her life, never fully recovering. Born a Baptist, before communism she had attended church and raised a happy, healthy family. But now, she was overcome by sadness. Ada recollects that she would always say, "My life ended a long time ago." She stopped going to church, stopped praying, and became listless. Driven to desperation by the murder machine of communism, she even had two abortions, an unthinkable act in her previous life. It is these invisible wounds that will never adequately be counted in the death toll of communism.

✠ ✠ ✠

Ada's grandparents on her mother's side were strong Catholics, always encouraging the children to pray the Rosary, receive the sacraments, and turn to each other for support.

By the 1980s, the situation for Romania's practicing Catholics resembled the white martyrdom of late Czechoslovakia. Citizens were "allowed" to go to church, but they would pay the hidden cost later. Your job application travel visa would be mysteriously denied, your apartment would become run down. Ada remembers her mother warning the children that there were spies everywhere. As a result, practice of the Faith became, as Ada remembers, "low key." Celebrations and devotions had to be private rather than public, holidays were toned down.

One exception to this shadow existence was the annual Pentecost pilgrimage to Csíksomlyó, a Hungarian pilgrimage site since the fifteenth or sixteenth century. Every year, thousands of people flocked to the shrine at this site. Like the shrine of Our Lady of Charity in El Cobre, Cuba, the Csíksomlyó pilgrimage site was never touched by the communists.

Ada believes this fact approaches the miraculous. In 1798, the local bishop had declared the statue miraculous after it survived several invasions from the Tatars and Turks. Likewise, Our Lady was protected during World War I, and from the Nazi and communist armies alike. Somehow, the statue has emerged unscathed every time enemies tore through her land.

Ada's family attended this pilgrimage throughout communist rule. It was an anchor in their year, a small act of public resistance to totalitarian control. She credits this pilgrimage with bolstering her family's faith when the future was bleak. Since the fall of communism, the pilgrimage has only grown, from the "Camino of Hungary" to an international event representing Catholic victory over the forces of darkness.

After Ada's family left Romania for the United States in 1989, the regime's days were limited. Romania underwent its own anti-communist revolution in December of that year. Unlike its peaceful counterparts in Czechoslovakia and Poland, the Romanian revolution was a violent coup d'états with a strong military component. Nicolae Ceaușescu and his wife, Elena, were tried and convicted of economic sabotage and genocide on December 25 and executed by firing squad that same day on international television.

As young as she was at the time, Ada remembers watching the Christmas Day execution with her family. The television, once a weapon of Ceaușescu, was now turned against him as a spotlight on his corruption, allowing millions to witness justice.

✠ ✠ ✠

Romania has made some effort to reconcile with its communist past, notably through a land repatriation program that returns property illegally seized by the state. Ada's family has received parts of her grandparents' estate, though the buildings have all been destroyed and the land scarred by the communists' misuse.

She returns to her homeland with her own family to attend the Csíksomlyó pilgrimage as often as possible. Ada notes that Hungary's national anthem is "like a prayer":

O God, bless the nation of Hungary

With Your grace and bounty
Extend over it Your guarding arm
During strife with its enemies
Long torn by ill fate
Bring upon it a time of relief
This nation has suffered for all sins
Of the past and of the future!

This verse is a fitting anthem for the Csíksomlyó pilgrimage, which places a strong emphasis on repentance, offering a plenary indulgence to participants. The pilgrimage remains the largest annual gathering in Romania.[75] Hundreds of thousands of pilgrims participated in the 2023 Pentecost pilgrimage, renewing the gifts of the Holy Spirit under Our Lady's mantle, victorious over communism once again.

---

[75] "Our Lady of Csíksomlyó Pilgrimage," Pilgrim-Info.com, https://www.pilgrim-info.com/csiksomlyo-pilgrimage/.

The miraculous statue of Csíksomlyó. Photos courtesy Ada Ban

Theresa Nagymihaly Rust was born in 1943 in Dorozsma, a small village on the outskirts of Szeged, a city in southeast Hungary. She was the eldest of three daughters born to a factory owner and his wife. Her parents had grown up as peasants, migrating seasonally for agricultural work. Determined to provide a better life for his children, her father Gaspar had developed a special method of re-purposing broken looms, and he now ran a textile factory, affording job opportunities to hundreds of workers in the neighboring town of Kiskundorozsma.

Theresa remembers the dirt roads of her hometown and the simple lifestyle of her family. The factory's signature pattern of red textile with white polka dots adorned their house. Theresa's mother Veronica, who went home to the Lord in 2022 at the age of 103, still decorated her bedroom with this nostalgic pattern.

Some of Theresa's earliest memories are of the Second World War. The family was living in Budapest at the time, hoping that the great cultural city would be spared by Allied bombing. It was not. As a toddler, Theresa would go outside as her mother hung laundry to dry in the depleted streets. The young Theresa, then too little to perceive the realities of war, would laugh and clap as bombed-out buildings burnt to the ground, delighting in the spectacle.

But the war would leave lasting marks on the innocent young mind, too. One time, she witnessed a soldier push her mother to the ground to protect her from the bombs. Years later, even when living in the United States, Theresa would huddle under the bed when she heard planes overhead.

When the war ended, Hungary was divided into Allied occupation zones but fell heavily under Soviet control. The domestic communist takeover would soon follow. By 1948, full-scale communist economic policies were being implemented. As a factory owner, Theresa's father was targeted. She remembers the slurs hurled at him: the reverberations of "capitalist mongrel pig" have stayed with her to this day. When the communist soldiers came to arrest him, they tore through the family's house, ripping open the closets and emptying drawers. Theresa vividly remembers the image of her mother's white dresses billowing in the wind before they fell into the mud from the second-floor balcony.

Theresa's father spent many days in jail before being hauled in front of a court for his class crimes. His employees, astonished at this turn of events, arrived en masse to the court to defend him. They each wore swatches of the factory's signature pattern of red and white polka dots in solidarity. In a small miracle, the court spared him because of this show of support from the workers. But his time in prison taught him that this would not be an isolated incident. "They will kill you," his new companions assured him. He vowed then and there that if he was released, he would flee Hungary, taking his family to freedom. He couldn't squander this chance.

The very night he was released, he rushed home and told his wife to pack as much as she could into just one suitcase. If it was obvious that the family was fleeing the country, they were more likely to be stopped and sent back. They could plausibly play off one suitcase as just a vacation or a family visit. These supplies had to last the family of five, including Theresa's eight-month-old baby sister, indefinitely.

Late that night, they embarked on the uncertain journey west. Theresa, now five years old, soon became very grown-up. Her baby sister was crying inconsolably. Theresa whispered, "Please don't cry. I'll take care of you," not knowing what she could possibly do.

Theresa soon gave into the tears as they snuck through the damp marshes. She couldn't understand why she was being punished. What had she done wrong? What had her father done wrong?

On the next leg of the journey, the family acquired an ox cart. Theresa and her sisters hid under the hay as her parents, dressed in worn clothes, drove the cart. If they were stopped, they would claim they were peasant farmers attending to their crops. The couple had also procured fake travel passes authorizing them to attend a fictitious wedding.

The journey was further complicated by the new boundaries of the partition zones. The rules were different in each one. They hoped they would make it to an American zone eventually. Given the tenuous geopolitical situation in the war's aftermath, crossing from one zone to another was a dangerous affair. The many miles of marshland were overseen by guard towers manned by heavily armed soldiers.

Another small miracle came for the family through the underground refugee network. Catholic nuns oversaw this endeavor. The nuns helped smuggle Hungarian children to safety in Austria, informing the parents that their destination was Linz. The parents were then on their own to get across the border. Theresa's parents entrusted their three daughters, even the baby, to the nuns. As they said goodbye, they knew it could be for the last time.

Theresa remembers little of the journey but recalls the anxiety at the refugee orphanage camp in Linz. She sat there with her sisters surrounded by all the other children. One by one, they were claimed by sets of parents, haggard from their own journeys. As the sun set, Theresa and her sisters were the last remaining children. At that moment, Theresa vowed to take care of her little sisters, no matter what.

Suddenly, they heard familiar voices. Her parents were here after all! Somehow, they had struggled across the border. Later, Theresa's mother would relate some of their misadventures — at one point, they had had to crawl under barbed wire. But she usually didn't want to talk about what she witnessed. The brutality of soldiers of all sides in the occupation zones was difficult to stomach.

✠ ✠ ✠

The family spent two years in a refugee camp in Salzburg. They had a small room and meager provisions, but they were together. One time, her father accidentally wandered into the French occupation zone. The French soldiers threatened to deport him back to Hungary. Theresa's mother sobbed, pleading with the French to let him stay. They relented, granting the family a new lease on life.

The couple applied for amnesty everywhere they could, but few countries were willing to take a family with such a young baby. The long sea journey to Australia, for example, was out of the question. Theresa's father scoured the Western newspapers every day, scrolling the classifieds for anyone who might have work available or could serve as an immigration sponsor. One day, he spotted a Hungarian name—Szücs—in an American paper. The Hungarian man was a notary public in Philadelphia. Such a professional would carry some weight. It was worth a try!

To his surprise, the notary public wrote back. With sponsorship in hand, the family was doubly lucky to make the quota for immigration to the United States—all five of them.

The family's last Christmas in Europe was spent in that Salzburg refugee camp. Theresa and her sisters marveled at the bright lights and the trees, delivered "by the angels" on Christmas Eve. It was this Christmas that Theresa learned her first English words, "Thank you," directed at a kind soldier who came bearing candy and gifts.

Theresa's dad made sure his children said their prayers—in Hungarian, German, French, *and* English. He was determined to assimilate into his new homeland. They departed for the port of Bremerhaven, and then sailed to a new life in the United States, where they became citizens in 1955.

As Theresa grew up, she learned of the horrors that befell her homeland. She read of Cardinal Mindszenty, imprisoned and tortured by the communists for the Faith. She feels incredibly blessed that, as harrowing as her escape from communism had been, she was spared these trials and allowed to practice her faith in the open. Her parents were completely unable to contact the family they left behind. If they had set foot in Hungary, they surely would have been arrested as deserters and traitors. When Theresa's mother's father died, her mother couldn't even go to the funeral or comfort her family. Theresa considers this loss of family to be the worst legacy of communism. When Theresa eventually visited her homeland decades later, these bonds had been completely severed. There was no one left to visit. She's not sure what became of them.

After living briefly in Philadelphia, the family eventually settled in Miami, where they received employment and support from Gesu Catholic Church, and the girls attended Catholic boarding schools. Theresa lives in Miami to this day. She has made a spiritual home for herself among the Cuban émigrés at St. Kieran's parish, bonding over their shared experiences under communism, their strong faith, and their love of American values. Theresa knows she owes her life to her guardian angel's protection, and to her mother's sacrifice and resolve. She marvels that her mother had the foresight to protect her children's physical safety — and, more importantly, their souls — from the impending communist threat. She honors her mother's legacy by living out her faith boldly in her beloved adopted country.

✠ ✠ ✠

Fr. Maurus Nemeth, O.S.B., was born in a small Hungarian village in 1937. His family lived a rural lifestyle as farmers and suffered the deprivations of the war like thousands of others.

His father was briefly interned by the Nazis in a concentration camp, but he was released before the communist takeover in 1947.

Maurus remembers waking up at four o'clock in the morning to get a spot in the bread lines throughout the 1950s.

Newspaper clipping featuring the Nagymihaly family when they gained United States citizenship in 1955. Theresa is at the far left.

He was given the chance to go to school in Budapest. Out of 1400 applicants for a few hundred spots, he was selected, and his family made moves for him to take this opportunity. The school was run by the new communist state, and it served, as he would find out, as a training ground for students bound for university in Moscow. The school was housed in a building stolen from the Sisters of Sioni, who had been expelled in the early years of the revolution.

The 1949 Greek Civil War sent a flood of Greek refugees over Hungary's borders, and so the school was repurposed again, this time as an orphanage. Maurus and the other older students were put in charge of orphans as "big brothers." Maurus shepherded a group of twenty-four.

Fr. Maurus traces the development of his vocation back to these formative years: "I believe that my vocation to become a teacher and eventually a monk in the order of Saint Benedict, where teaching is emphasized,... really sprouted there in those three years."

The practice of religion was completely forbidden. But Maurus had been raised a strong Catholic, and knew that his duties to God overrode any duties to the state. He and a few classmates had Sunday afternoons off. They plotted their escape for hours, marking off on a map all the churches they had already visited so they wouldn't arouse suspicion by attending the same parish twice. Every Sunday, they would sneak to a different church in the city of Budapest, receiving the sacraments in secret.

Bu they hadn't covered their tracks as well as they thought.

In February 1956, several months before the Hungarian Revolution, they were called to the office of the headmaster. The party secretary of the entire district was there. "They were ready to kick us out!" Maurus recalls. "Just three months before our graduation." After a prolonged period they were granted clemency because of their strong record of helping the orphans, but the consequences would catch up with them later. The students would not be able to get into any higher education institution. Maurus had been vying for the medical school in Budapest, but now the answer was absolutely no.

He didn't give up hope. He returned home to spend time with his parents and volunteered in a hospital, doing odd jobs and soaking up as much information and experience as he could. He had an uncle in medicine — maybe he could pull some strings.

Soon, however, the revolution would interrupt those plans.

In October 1956, Maurus was on the streets of Budapest when Soviet tanks rolled in, escalating a peaceful protest to violent chaos. Maurus joyfully marched with his friends, finally able to make some sort of stand against the oppressive system.

He hadn't thought that anyone would take any notice, given the raucous atmosphere and popular participation. But a month later, his former math teacher, whom Maurus had always thought of as a friend, approached him. "Make a choice," he warned: East or West. His actions had not gone unnoticed. Unless he was prepared to put his head down and show loyalty to the state, he would have to flee or else face almost certain imprisonment.

He chose to escape. It was a sudden decision, but the revolution had changed everything. Firm in his resolve, he vowed to see his parents one more time.

He and several friends went down from Budapest to his hometown, providentially located near the Austrian border. He told his parents of his plan. His mother's tears struck him to the core. He didn't want to leave. But staying was impossible. "Finally they understood, although I don't think they could accept it," he reminisces. His family had certainly suffered under communism: his father had been captured by the communists and pressed into forced labor at a camp, just as he had been under the Nazis just years before. In both cases, he had managed to escape. But the situation was tenuous.

The night of November 28, around midnight, the group of refugees approached the river with a little boat. They tiptoed along the bank, knowing that mines—from the war, and to prevent escape—dotted the shoreline.

Flares lit up the sky on the opposite side of the river. This was a good sign: Maurus had heard that there were people in Austria who were helping thousands of Hungarians escape by these very means. They made it across almost without incident, and walked up a snowy hill into freedom. On the other side, the denizens of the small Austrian village were waiting with hot tea.

Maurus and his friends spent the next three months in a refugee camp. Like Theresa's family, all the refugees were training for amnesty applications. Maurus recalls being drilled in English, every word moving them closer to the promised land of the United States and Canada.

Maurus was selected to be part of a special group and travel to Holland as "the guests of the queen." From there, he applied for and was granted amnesty in Canada. When he got to Canada, he took any job he could get, from seasonal agricultural labor to logging to manual labor on the railroad.

He eventually settled in Vancouver where, much to his delight, he found a community of Hungarian expats who joined forces to build a Catholic church. The parish life flourished in a way he had never been able to experience under the constant surveillance in communist Hungary. He had not forgotten the medical profession, but his vocation to the religious life was rekindled here. In search of a priest for their newly built community, he visited the Woodside Priory of Saint Anselm College in California, where many Hungarian refugees were living out their Benedictine vocations. "The rest is history!" he laughs. In the Benedictine vocation, he would find an outlet for his passion for medicine and mentorship, teaching biology for forty-three years.

Now ordained, Fr. Maurus began making return trips to Hungary. In 1972, he arrived in Budapest only to be ordered to report directly to the police station. A tall police colonel looked him in the eye. "I know who you are. I'm going to ask you a few questions," he snapped. "And I know everything about you," he continued, gesturing to the thick dossier on the table in front of him. "You'd better tell me the truth!"

Fr. Maurus squarely responded: "Sir, if you know everything about me, you also know that I am a Benedictine monk, studying to be a priest. I am not in the business of lying. Go ahead and ask your questions."

And he did. One by one, he pulled all the letters that Fr. Maurus had written home during those years from his folder. The agent knew every detail of Fr. Maurus's life, even after he escaped

Hungary — exactly where he was in Canada, when he came to California, and all the rest.

Then, he started to ask about Fr. Maurus's friends. Fr. Maurus interrupted: "Sir, you can ask anything you want about me, and I will answer you. But you have no right to ask me about anyone else, and if you do, I won't tell you."

The colonel backed off.

After the collapse of communism, many formerly communist states have made these state security files available for viewing. Some people choose not to view their own file, as it often contains hurtful answers they would rather keep unknown. The countless revelations of father spying on son, brother on brother, have ripped families apart.

Fr. Maurus continues to travel back to his beloved homeland, where he keeps in touch with his sister, who was just eight years old when he escaped. He organizes pilgrimages and an exchange program, facilitating understanding of Hungary's recent history.

"It was a ... little life story, not an important one, but I can say where Almighty God was good to me, and [if the] Good Lord [asked] if I would want to start it again, I happily would say yes!"

CONCLUSION

When the Sickle Swings

Memory, Meaning, and Martyrdom

SOMETIMES HISTORY SUPPLIES us with such supreme ironies that all words fail. Such is the case with the hammer and sickle, the ubiquitous iconography of communism.

It is fitting that the sickle, a timeless symbol of death across cultures, was enshrined in communism as a celebration of the fruits of this life, which are death. The sickle, as a representation of agricultural work, indicates the moment at which the grain is cut down—to be processed, refined, purified, and transformed into something life-giving. I can think of no more perfect metaphor for the martyrs who were cut down by the sickle of communism, their sacrifices uniting with Christ's in giving lifeblood to the Church.

The hammer, while also meant to represent physical labor, calls to mind the hammer of judgment. The mockery that communism made of justice—the pageant of show trials and false tribunals that condemned the innocent to imprisonment and execution—is a black mark on the perpetrators' souls. Calling to mind the inverted "justice" that was used to condemn Our Lord to death, it will be held in judgment against them at the only tribunal that matters: the final judgment before the throne of God.

✠ ✠ ✠

What sets the Catholic martyrs of communism apart from countless others who needlessly suffered since 1917 is the language, substance, and understanding of martyrdom.

In the aftermath of the traumatic twentieth century, much has been written about memory and meaning-making. Many innocents who suffered at the hands of both Nazi and communist regimes have processed their experiences through writing, developing a worldview that makes sense of their brutal, unfair, and often arbitrary ordeals.

Foremost among these is Viktor Frankl's *Man's Search for Meaning*, in which he develops his system of *logotherapy* in response to his agony at Auschwitz. Logotherapy is a psychological approach that allows a sufferer to employ his "will to meaning," a concept developed by the Danish philosopher Søren Kierkegaard.

Frankl's book and others have given rise to an entire genre of genocide memoir that demonstrate in real time the beautiful restoration of the pieces of broken lives. Elie Wiesel's narrative *Night* employs storytelling and vignette to communicate his experience and foster healing. Primo Levi's Auschwitz memoirs use the lens of science to interpret his imprisonment. Memoirs are such a useful genre because they so often reveal undercurrents of philosophy, religion, and culture, and how these color actions and identity.

Reflecting the broader philosophical schools of nihilism and absurdism, some memoirists have concluded that there *is* no meaning. That suffering is arbitrary, chaotic, and impossible to integrate. This interpretation often leads to despair.

These ideologies are essentially immanent—that is, the meaning arises from the suffering, *a posteriori*. The task of meaning-making falls to the individual. He must develop a transcendent gestalt to superimpose upon his life, a program of interpretation through which to pass the raw material of his life.

Books such as Frankl's and Wiesel's are beautiful examples of the resilience of the human spirit, the power of forgiveness, and the importance of inner peace. But there is still something missing: grace. It is clear that the only way to hold on to one's humanity after undergoing such trauma is to imbue this suffering with meaning. Catholicism provides a built-in, *a priori* blueprint for meaningful suffering, authored by God Himself. The vocation of every Catholic is martyrdom, be it red or white. At our Baptism, we die to this world, rendering all utopian worldly promises meaningless. At every moment—from a minor inconvenience to the sacrifice of our lives—we have the opportunity to unite our suffering to Christ's and give it eternal weight. Offering up suffering turns temporary pain into *eternal* glory.

For many of the persecuted, their experiences prompt them to discover or rekindle their faith, as we saw in this book with the prisoners of La Cabaña. This is also the case with Aleksandr Solzhenitsyn. His landmark memoir *The Gulag Archipelago* stands out from other writing in this meaning-making genre not only in the majesty of his writing and scope but also because of his recognition of the infusion of supernatural grace. Relieved of the responsibility to make sense of it all, he allowed *God* to be the one to author the significance of his own life.

The people in this book understood this surrender to God's will and the power of efficacious suffering. Sometimes, the fruits of their struggles came to fruition in this world: the Velvet Revolution and toppling of communism in Eastern Europe. Sometimes the temporal aims were frustrated: the Bay of Pigs Invasion. Often, the progress seems meaningless in worldly terms: the absurdity of the bureaucratic wild goose chases in Czechoslovakia.

But as the increasing number of canonizations indicates, the fruits of these sufferings in the next life are abundant.

✠ ✠ ✠

Even in this world, the fruits of these lives are to be found in their heroic example of absolute, uncompromising adherence to the Catholic Faith.

Fr. Martin Jugie writes in his treatise on Purgatory that the act of writing one good Catholic book will reverberate in eternity, gaining graces for the author as he ascends to Heaven. How much more, then, will the act of a life lived in heroic virtue edify the faithful and therefore assist these souls?

If only one person reads this book and is inspired to become more convicted in the Faith, to stand up to injustice, then the sacrifices of these individuals will be exponentially magnified before the throne of God.

Just as saints serve as icons of God's grace, so too are heroic stories of Catholics in our own time meant to be told. They serve as living icons of God's grace. Their stories are meant for the edification of the faithful. As opposed to the false, impoverished fraternity of communism, we are united to their sufferings by virtue of our membership in the Mystical Body of Christ.

The diversity of the saints shows that fidelity to God comes in many forms, some more dramatic than others, but all leading to the same place: Heaven. From the violent martyrdoms of the apostles to the quiet sanctity of St. Thérèse, all that God asks of us is a radical surrender to His particular will for our lives.

Stories of survivors of communism reflect the same pattern: whether their lives consisted of red or white martyrdom, their decisions at each juncture show us that we too can resist the institutionalized forces of evil with small, daily actions.

In this book there is a story relatable to each of us. While we may not have the opportunity for such extraordinary action, we can be inspired by these witnesses to exemplify the same virtues in our ordinary lives. There is no such thing as *ordinary* to God. God intends Heaven for each of us, and allows us to face challenges to that end.

✠ ✠ ✠

As time marches on, we are becoming further distant from the realities of communism, although its godless principles are still found in governments today.

On the whole, memorialization of communist atrocities has become more important. Several notable organizations have taken on this work. Foremost among them is the Victims of Communism Memorial Foundation in Washington, D.C.

In addition to the forwarding of causes for canonization, memorialization projects from within the Church have taken the form of public monuments, shrines, and personal devotions. In recent years, there has been a flourishing of the publication of memoirs from this period.

✠ ✠ ✠

The Czech Republic and Slovakia, as Mikloško discussed, are slowly coming to terms with both their Nazi-occupied and communist-occupied pasts. Poland has likewise made great strides in this area. But in some countries, memorialization has been shaky at best. Across Eastern Europe, progress is being made, with some major setbacks.

Just last year, the Russian government forcibly shut down the human rights advocacy group Memorial, a longtime witness to the victims of the Gulag. Journalist Masha Gessen's moving book of photojournalism *Never Remember* chronicles Russia's tacit gag order on full and proper remembrance of the Gulag.[76] She discovers the pervading attitude that moving on as a nation means simply not bothering with an unpleasant past: "The cacophony conveys the sense that the Gulag meant everything and nothing. That is the distinguishing characteristic of the Putin-era historiography of Soviet terror. It says, in effect, that it just happened, whatever."[77]

✠ ✠ ✠

Beyond commemoration of the past, the Church faces the continued challenges of active communist regimes in the present. The faithful today face the same struggles described in this book, albeit in different contexts.

The Church continues to grow in Vietnam, despite the machinations of the reigning communist government.

While the Church in Cuba is officially under the auspices of Rome, with its own cardinals and clergy, the situation remains fraught, contending against government interference and the continued influence of liberation theology. The same Communist Party that killed Rogelio Gonzalez Corzo still runs Cuba to this day. It remains an open-air island prison of repression and poverty that penalizes the virtuous.

The Church in China suffers under the same "national church" farce that earned the Czechoslovak national church an excommunication—increasingly, with the Vatican's approval. The ongoing persecution of Cardinal Zen, and Rome's silence, speak volumes.

In North Korea, what remains of the Catholic Church has become completely nationalized. The Democratic People's Republic

---

[76] Masha Gessen, *Never Remember: Searching for Stalin's Gulags in Putin's Russia* (New York: Columbia Global Reports, 2018), 108.

[77] Ibid.

of Korea claims that several hundred souls belong to the state-run "Korean Catholic Association." The episcopal sees have remained vacant since the violent persecutions of Catholics in the 1940s.

Historian of the Gulag Stephen Cohen writes, in his book *The Victims Return*, "As we know from other historical atrocities, crimes like Stalin's leave behind survivors who will bear witness even in the face of state repression."[78] He then goes on to quote Russian historian Vladlen Loginov on the new way in which history must be done in order to match the lack of traditional sources: "Every era gives rise to its own specific types of sources."[79]

Under such duress, when governments are literally destroying evidence, faking numbers, and barring historians from primary sources, the sources are the *people themselves* who bore witness. Telling the truth becomes a radical act of resistance and preservation. The practice of oral history and interviewing has taken on a new importance in memorializing these stories.

No one is obligated to tell their story, to the world or even to their family. For many, what they went through is too private and too painful, and they focus on prayer and healing.

For each story represented in this book, there are millions more. For the scope of this book, I was only able to profile a handful of countries, and the stories, while representative, are necessarily incomplete. We may never know the full scope of communist oppression of the Catholic Church. Untold numbers of Catholics lost their lives at the hands of the communists and never had a chance to tell their stories. Many more survived communism and have since

---

[78] Stephen F. Cohen, *The Victims Return: Survivors of the Gulag after Stalin* (London: I. B. Tauris, 2012).

[79] Ibid., 24.

passed away. Survivors who remain are aging, with little time left to record their deeds before they disappear into the silence of history.

If you or someone you know survived communism, I urge you to tell your story. I hope to make it my life's work to record these important testimonies for the sake of justice, posterity, and witness to the Faith. No story is too small or insignificant: together they weave a tapestry of multifaceted resilience in the face of horror.

✠ ✠ ✠

It is evident that communism, which Pius XI excoriated as "contrary to reason and divine revelation," has been and continues to be the agent of horrific anti-Catholic persecution. But in the midst of this suffering come tremendous graces. The blood of martyrs is the seed of the Church.

We never know what God will ask of us. Each of us is tested in our own unique ways. Given the climate of the world today, it is increasingly possible that our faith will be tested in extreme ways, as it was for the people in this book. We are hurtling toward the apocalypse. Be it months, years, or centuries, the end of the world approaches.

But we do know two inevitable outcomes that we will certainly face: our death and personal judgment, and the final judgment. Each of our actions will be brought before the tribunal of God, the only judge who matters. We all yearn to hear "Well done, good and faithful servant."

The question is not *if* the sickle will swing, but *when*. When the sickle swings—be it of a communist regime, the antichrist himself, or the angel of death—we must be ready.

Selected Bibliography

Catholics under Communism: General

Corley, Felix. *Religion in the Soviet Union: An Archival Reader.* New York: New York University Press, 1993.

Dreher, Rod. *Live Not by Lies: A Manual for Christian Dissidents.* New York: Sentinel, 2020.

Kengor, Paul. *The Devil and Karl Marx: Communism's Long March of Death, Deception, and Infiltration.* Gastonia, NC: TAN Books, 2020.

————— *The Antichrist.* West Hanover, MA: Christopher, 1981).

Miceli, Vincent, S.J. *The Gods of Atheism.* Manchester, NH: Sophia Institute Press, 2022.

Murray, Damon, and Stephen Sorrell, eds. *Godless Utopia: Soviet Anti-Religious Propaganda.* London: FUEL, 2019.

Nicholas, Mary A., and Paul Kengor. *The Devil and Bella Dodd: One Woman's Struggle against Communism and Her Redemption.* Gastonia, NC: TAN Books, 2022.

Cuba

Betto, Frei, and Fidel Castro. *Fidel and Religion: Conversations with Frei Betto on Marxism and Liberation Theology.* North Melbourne, Australia: Ocean Press, 2006.

Fernández-Travieso, Tomás. *Beyond the Silence.* Scotts Valley, CA: Createspace, 2015.

Gutiérrez-Boronat, Orlando. *Cuba: The Doctrine of the Lie.* Washington, DC: Academica Press, 2022.

Triay, Victor. *Bay of Pigs: An Oral History of Brigade 2506.* Gainesville: University Press of Florida, 2001.

——— *Fleeing Castro: Operation Pedro Pan and the Cuban Children's Program.* Gainesville: University Press of Florida, 1999.

Tweed, Thomas A. *Our Lady of the Exile: Diasporic Religion at a Cuban Catholic Shrine in Miami.* New York: Oxford University Press, 1997.

Valladares, Armando. *Against All Hope: A Memoir of Life in Castro's Gulag.* Translated by Andrew Hurley. New York: Encounter Books, 2001.

Czechoslovakia

Corley, Felix. "The Secret Clergy in Communist Czechoslovakia." *Religion, State and Society* 21, no. 2 (1993): 171–206, https://doi.org/10.1080/09637499308431590.

Gansrigler, Franz. *Jeder War Ein Papst: Geheimkirchen in Osteuropa.* [Every man a pope: The secret Church in Eastern Europe.] Salzburg: Otto Müller, 1991.

Halík, Tomáš. *From the Underground Church to Freedom.* Translated by Gerald Turner. Notre Dame, IN: University of Notre Dame Press, 2019.

Hungary/Romania

Mindszenty, József Cardinal. *Memoirs.* Translated by Richard and Clara Winstn. New York: Macmillan, 1974.

Zoltan, M. "A csíksomlyói kegyhely legendaköre" (Legends of the Csíksomlyó shrine). *Ethnographia* 127, no. 2 (2016): 212–225.

Other Countries

Alliluyeva, Svetlana. *Only One Year: A Memoir.* New York: Harper Perennial, 2017.

Ciszek, Walter J., S.J., and Daniel L. Flaherty, S.J. *He Leadeth Me.* New York: Image, 2014.

——— *With God in Russia.* San Francisco: Ignatius Press, 1997.

Efimova, Miroslava. *Harsh Vineyard: A History of Catholic Life in the Russian Far East.* Victoria, British Columbia: Trafford, 2008.

Fazzini, Gerolamo, ed. *Diaries of the Chinese Martyrs: Stories of Heroic Catholics Living in Mao's China.* Translated by Charlotte J. Fasi. Manchester, NH: Sophia Institute Press, 2016.

Jubani, Dom Simon. *From the Depths of Hell I Saw Jesus on the Cross: A Priest in the Prisons of Communist Albania.* Translated by Angelo Massafra and Joseph Bamberg. Waterloo, Ontario: Arouca Press, 2021.

Stabinska, Jadwiga. *For Their Sake I Consecrate Myself: Sister Maria Bernadette of the Cross.* Translated by Justyna Krukowska. Waterloo, Ontario: Arouca Press, 2022.

Zugger, Christopher. *The Forgotten: Catholics of the Soviet Empire from Lenin through Stalin.* Syracuse, NY: Syracuse University Press, 2001.

Memory Studies and Communism in General

Adler, Nanci. *Keeping Faith with the Party: Communist Believers Return from the Gulag.* Bloomington: Indiana University Press, 2012.

———— *The Gulag Survivor: Beyond the Soviet System.* New Brunswick, NJ: Transaction, 2004.

Cohen, Stephen F. *The Victims Return: Survivors of the Gulag After Stalin.* London: I. B. Tauris, 2012.

Funder, Anna. *Stasiland: Stories from behind the Berlin Wall.* New York: Harper Perennial, 2011.

Shalamov, Varlam. *Kolyma Stories.* Translated by Donald Rayfield. New York: New York Review Books, 2018.

Solzhenitsyn, Aleksandr. *The Gulag Archipelago, 1918–1956.* Translated by Thomas P. Whitney. New York: Westview Press, 1991–1992.

Image Credits

Polo Aguilera holds the crucifix he has treasured since grade school, courtesy of the author (taken by friend).

The author with Polo Aguilera in his Miami home, courtesy of the author (taken by friend).

A rosary carved by a Cuban political prisoner from a cigar box, Bay of Pigs Museum, Miami, taken by author.

Two wood rosaries made by hand in prison, Bay of Pigs Museum, Miami, taken by author.

Scapulars worn in the political prisons of Cuba, Bay of Pigs Museum, Miami, taken by author.

The author with members of Brigade 2506, veterans of the Bay of Pigs invasion who now operate the Bay of Pigs Museum in Miami, and Historian Victor Triay, taken by author.

The Brigade 2506 Logo adorns the museum's façade, taken by author.

The original flag of Brigade 2506, returned by President John F. Kennedy to the Brigade upon its amnesty in December 1962, taken by author.

Our Lady of Charity image at the Miami Shrine, taken by author.

Bishop Agustin Roman of Miami, taken by author.

Bp. Roman's clerical apparel, taken by author.

Sunflowers: the symbols of freedom, taken by author.

Pilgrims bring sunflowers to Our Lady of Charity, taken by author.

Dios, Patria, y Vida, the motto of the Cuban diaspora, courtesy Frantisek Miklosko.

The Miklosko family in the early 1950s. Frantisek kneels in front, courtesy Frantisek Miklosko.

The Kalvaria at Nitra, Slovakia, c. 1950s, courtesy Frantisek Miklosko.

Crosses adorn the hill at Kalvaria, Nitra, courtesy Frantisek Miklosko.

Frantisek Miklosko with Cardinal Tomasek, Bishop Jan Korec, and Jan Carnogursky, courtesy Frantisek Miklosko.

Bishop Jan Korec in his apartment with the anti-eavesdropping apparatus he used to communicate with friends and allies, courtesy Frantisek Miklosko.

Vladimir Jukl after his release from thirteen-and-a-half years in prison in 1965, courtesy Frantisek Miklosko.

Miklosko attends an outing with the youth of the underground Church, courtesy Frantisek Miklosko.

Miklosko attends an outing with the youth of the underground Church, courtesy Frantisek Miklosko.

Miklosko's graduation from Comenius University in Bratislava, 1971, courtesy Frantisek Miklosko.

Miklosko and Bp. Korec at the Nitra Pilgrimage for the feast of Our Lady's Assumption, 1988, courtesy Frantisek Miklosko.

Miklosko and Bp. Korec at the Nitra Pilgrimage for the feast of Our Lady's Assumption, 1989, courtesy Frantisek Miklosko.

Pope John Paul II receives Vladimir Jukl, courtesy Frantisek Miklosko.

The Csiklomyo Pilgrimage, courtesy Ada Ban.

Statue of Our Lady at Csiklomyo, courtesy Ada Ban.

Miami Herald article commemorating the Nagymihaly family's American citizenship, courtesy Theresa Rust.

About the Author

KRISTEN VAN UDEN began this project as an undergraduate at Saint Anselm College, where she earned a B.A. in history and Russian area studies. She trained in oral history and began researching the experience of Catholics who survived, escaped, or resisted communist regimes.

She then worked as an apprentice in oral history at the Earl Gregg Swem Library's Special Collections Research Center at the College of William & Mary, where she completed her M.A. in history.

She researches Catholics who survived totalitarianism in the twentieth century. She is especially interested in pursuing this subject through the historiographies of Catholic martyrdom, memory studies, and dissident literature.

She currently works at Sophia Institute Press as a media spokesperson, and has been featured on a wide variety of media platforms such as *First Things*, Sensus Fidelium, and Coast to Coast AM. She is also the editor of Catholic Exchange.

Sophia Institute

SOPHIA INSTITUTE IS a nonprofit institution that seeks to nurture the spiritual, moral, and cultural life of souls and to spread the gospel of Christ in conformity with the authentic teachings of the Roman Catholic Church.

Sophia Institute Press fulfills this mission by offering translations, reprints, and new publications that afford readers a rich source of the enduring wisdom of mankind.

Sophia Institute also operates the popular online resource CatholicExchange.com. *Catholic Exchange* provides world news from a Catholic perspective as well as daily devotionals and articles that will help readers to grow in holiness and live a life consistent with the teachings of the Church.

In 2013, Sophia Institute launched Sophia Institute for Teachers to renew and rebuild Catholic culture through service to Catholic education. With the goal of nurturing the spiritual, moral, and cultural life of souls, and an abiding respect for the role and work of teachers, we strive to provide materials and programs that are at once enlightening to the mind and ennobling to the heart; faithful and complete, as well as useful and practical.

Sophia Institute gratefully recognizes the Solidarity Association for preserving and encouraging the growth of our apostolate over the course of many years. Without their generous and timely support, this book would not be in your hands.

www.SophiaInstitute.com
www.CatholicExchange.com
www.SophiaInstituteforTeachers.org

Sophia Institute Press is a registered trademark of Sophia Institute.
Sophia Institute is a tax-exempt institution as defined by the
Internal Revenue Code, Section 501(c)(3). Tax ID 22-2548708.